Black, Brown, Bruised

Black, Brown, Bruised

*How Racialized STEM Education
Stifles Innovation*

Ebony Omotola McGee

HARVARD EDUCATION PRESS
CAMBRIDGE, MASSACHUSETTS

Second Printing, 2021

Paperback ISBN 978-1-68253-535-6
Library Edition ISBN 978-1-68253-536-3

Library of Congress Cataloging-in-Publication Data is on file.

Published by Harvard Education Press,
an imprint of the Harvard Education Publishing Group
Harvard Education Press
8 Story Street
Cambridge, MA 02138

Cover Design: Ciano Design
Cover Image: smartboy10/DigitalVision Vectors via Getty Images

The typefaces in this book are ITC Stone Serif for text and
Stone Sans for display.

DEDICATION

*This book is dedicated to my African ancestors
for originating many fields of study—mathematics,
astronomy, chemistry, engineering, navigation,
maritime technology, metallurgy, architecture,
abstract art, medicine, immunizations, surgery,
textiles, farming, and agronomy—as well as
writing, calendars, libraries, universities,
music, art, the relationship between
science and spirituality,
and so much more.*

*To Khari:
Keep rollin son . . . onward and upward!*

The idea of being able to do something I love and help others realize their dreams, it's the perfect solution for me, the perfect dream.

—*Ashanti Johnson, geochemist and chemical oceanographer*

The way to approach it [the topic of race], I think, is not to ask, "What would it be like to be black?" but to seriously consider what it is like to be white. That's something white people almost never think about. And what it is like to be white is not to say, "We have to level the playing field," but to acknowledge that not only do white people own the playing field but they have so designated this plot of land as a playing field to begin with. White people *are* the playing field. The advantage of being white is so extreme, so overwhelming, that to use the word "advantage" at all is misleading since it implies a kind of parity that simply does not exist.

—*Fran Lebowitz*

Don't let anyone rob you of your imagination, your creativity, or your curiosity. It's your place in the world; it's your life. Go on and do all you can with it, and make it the life you want to live.

—*Mae Jemison, first African American woman astronaut in space*

CONTENTS

A Treatise for the Punished Pushed to an Imminent Rebellion

DR. EBONY OMOTOLA MCGEE has charged me with the responsibility of offering some opening words. In response to her call, I am reminded of the work of critical science educator, researcher, and scholar Daniel Morales-Doyle in that we rarely take into account the idea that mainstream White society still maintains its hold on who is allowed to be a scientist. By the time a Black or Latinx youth reaches second grade and expresses an interest in science, we cut their dreams short and write it off as impossible given their conditions (structural racism, poverty, low test scores, disinvested schools, etc.).

When we think of the preparation, study, and commitment to trial and error required to engage for inquiry into the natural, physical, and medical sciences, rarely do we think of Black and Latinx youth as potentially having the solutions to address their conditions. In worst-case scenarios, scholars Nicole Nguyen, Sepehr Vakil, and Shirin Vossoughi inform us on how STEM, in some instances, is utilized to usher students of color, particularly those from historically marginalized and isolated communities, into the war economy by way of the military industrial complex. As science is weaponized to combat concerns like "international terrorism" (via Homeland Security institutes at the high school level), the same technologies are used domestically on Black and Latinx communities to justify surveillance and occupation (e.g., war or drugs, war on crime, war on gangs, etc.). Again, Black and Brown folks are asked to produce and/or justify the same violent mechanisms that are used against them in the name of science. To some, STEM or STEAM (A is added for art to the science, technology, engineering, and mathematics moniker for good measure) has solidified itself as yet another tool by which to sort the have-nots from the chosen.

I am pleased to state that the offering *Black, Brown, Bruised: How Racialized STEM Education Stifles Innovation* seeks to challenge the aforementioned realities. Where some may think my comments to be a harsh and unfair critique of STEM or STEAM, I remind them that my writing of this document takes place during a global health pandemic. The novel coronavirus COVID-19 (SARS-CoV-2) has spread across countries and continents, exposing those who have historically been deemed disposable to the worst of its wrath. This moment is not only timely and relevant to *Black, Brown, Bruised* currently, but will remain salient for the foreseeable future for the following reasons. First, this moment has laid bare societal disparities along the lines of race, class, gender, age, (dis)ability, and sexual orientation that have existed for time immemorial. Second, and into the distant future, STEM education will make a pivot to pay specific attention to the prevention and containment of pandemics, prioritizing disciplines that engage environmental and medical sciences. As *Black, Brown, Bruised* dares to propose suggestions on how to address the prevalence of White supremacy in STEM-related education in colleges and universities, it is also providing a road map to open the gates to those who potentially have the answers for some of humanity's most pressing concerns.

Given Dr. McGee's dedication to poignantly illuminate the totalizing power of White supremacy in STEM education, the assumed views and values of White, Western European–descended, cis-gender, heterosexual, protestant, able-bodied males as normal, right, and good while othering everything else (White supremacy) are challenged explicitly. If we understand White supremacy as one of the baseline realities in STEM education, it becomes easier to embrace radical imaginaries like those of Dr. McGee that push us to work with others to change the current condition.

I have to admit, I envision many reading the previous paragraph and saying, *"Why can't we just have a conversation about the promise and possibility of STEM?"* To their question, I would reply, *"It is impossible to talk about any possibility of STEM in the current moment and for the long haul without an explicit acknowledgment of the totalizing power of White supremacy."* Currently in Chicago, almost 70 percent of deaths from COVID-19 have been Black folks. As schools have been forced to shutter their doors, many have limited or no access to reliable Wi-Fi networks, computers, or tablets. Before the shelter-in-place orders issued by local and state governments, 60 percent of young people in Chicago Public Schools (CPS) accessed the internet via their phones. These are the people who are structurally marginalized from STEM education. Dr. McGee, as a Chicago Southsider herself, understands these realties while revealing the consequences of not valuing Black, Brown, and Indigenous minds and bodies. *Black, Brown, Bruised* is fearless in its understanding of these realities while uplifting the necessity of prioritizing the needs of people who come from these conditions who are entering STEM fields in colleges and universities.

Years ago, I would ask my high school students in the beginning of the year if they had ever been punished for not reading or doing math well. It would always surprise me how many of my students answered yes. Reflecting on it now, I realize that I was really asking them to confirm my own trauma given my struggles with math. I can remember dismissing myself as "not good" at math and isolating myself, refusing to engage in math-centered activities. When I got to high school, I was surprised by what was expected of me in my math classes. As I started to talk to my classmates, I began to realize that the things I was doing in eighth-grade math were done by my classmates in their fourth- and fifth-grade classes. Because I didn't conceptualize the fact that they had a different set of resources regarding math instruction, I just wrote it off as them being "smarter" than me. Instead, it confirms the fact that this has never been an aptitude issue as much as it is a resource issue. Pushing us forward, *Black, Brown, Bruised* challenges us to entertain the questions *STEM for what? STEM for whom? How can the skills learned in STEM programming be used to develop tangible mechanisms for changing the conditions of my community and the people I care about?* In the end, I think science will be appreciative of these subjective questions.

We have to come to grips with the fact that we still ask young people to suffer through their university experiences in STEM education, with the hope that they won't ask deeper questions of its relevance and utility. Science, technology, engineering, (art), and mathematics *might* present an avenue to rupture the orthodoxy of White supremacy in STEM, but it will only do so if paired with critical analysis and fugitive planning. *Black, Brown, Bruised* digs deeper into the challenge of making sure that the justice-minded Black, Latinx, and Indigenous scholars have a way to build what we need. The current state of affairs (before and after the pandemic) remains unacceptable. I know that more orthodoxy won't give us the answers we need. Instead, we need to consider whether or not STEM, STEAM, or any iteration has the power to shift the paradigm.

As disruptive work, I understand *Black, Brown, Bruised* to operate in the spirit of Katherine Johnson, Ellen Ochoa, and Susan La Flesche Picotte. Because Dr. McGee has dared to be unpopular and has named the devil in the room concerning the exclusion of Black, Brown, and Indigenous folks in the physical, natural and medical sciences, engineering, technology, and mathematics, it is important that we support her fugitive and revolutionary praxis. Given the responsibility placed on me by Dr. McGee, it is my humble prayer that these words reflect solidarity with her efforts.

David Omotoso Stovall, PhD
Chicago
April 22, 2020

The URM
Student Experience
in STEM

FOR YEARS, I HAVE ASKED my research participants what it means to be Black or Latinx as they study science, technology, engineering, and mathematics, or STEM. Although it is useful to investigate why these underrepresented, racially minoritized (URM) students do not find success in STEM majors, I have concentrated on understanding those who do academically succeed. Studying and problematizing traditional notions of academic success enables a deep appreciation of what it means for students of color to be academically successful in places where their numbers are few and negative beliefs about their ability prevail.

As Black, Indigenous, and Latinx students brave the chilly waters of White-dominated STEM universities, certain experiences crop up regularly: isolation, feeling or being positioned as an impostor, and racial stereotypes and other forms of racialized bias that distract URM students from their studies and sap their energy. These URM students find it hard to establish relationships with faculty who do not share their racial identity or maybe its vice versa. Their advisers are usually White or Asian and do not understand what the students are going through.[1] Many URM students do not have mentors and are not privy to understanding the full benefit from receiving support from a mentor or how to find a mentor. Without these faculty advocates, they face limited learning opportunities and miss out on academic programs such as studying abroad and tuition-paid research assistant positions. Faculty and peers can be covertly or openly racist, engaging in discriminatory, passive-aggressive behavior, and stereotyping.[2] As a result, URM students cope with outsize stress that has psychological, physical, and academic effects, and they drop out of STEM programs at higher rates than their White and Asian counterparts. Intersectional issues, such as those experienced by a Black trans woman or a gay, Indigenous wheelchair user, heighten all these difficulties, often adding misogynistic, anti-LGBTQ+, and antidisability discrimination to race-based barriers.

In this book, I clarify how the path to success for all URM students remains challenging, even for those at the top of the STEM academic ladder and, surprisingly, even at historically Black colleges and universities (HBCUs) and Hispanic-serving institutions (HSIs). URM doctoral students at HBCUs and HSIs tell me that their STEM professors are mostly Asian or European, and at the graduate and postdoctoral levels, the students are largely international. One postdoctoral scholar in mechanical engineering at an HBCU reported that the primarily international Asian faculty, doctoral students, and postdoctoral researchers at her institution referred to Black students as "under-intelligent." In attempts to prove Black students' inferiority, some faculty and peers would attempt to sabotage Black students' research projects. In this hostile environment, one postdoctoral scholar felt that any behavior that diverged from what these racist people deemed acceptable would reflect negatively on the entire Black race:

That representation piece is key, because a lot of times, some of the classes I struggled in, I struggled in because I didn't want to go to the professor's office hours, or I felt like the professor was unreachable. I felt like maybe I had to kind of seem strong, and maybe visiting office hours would be seen as a sign of weakness or something like that. I just felt like, by going to their office hours, they would make me feel dumb or they wouldn't listen to me as a person and they would just say, "See? These Black kids can't cut it."

The strain of being in this untenable position is obvious. If that's how it is in graduate schools, including some that were founded to serve Black students, how much worse is it in a university founded with profits from slave trading or one whose students and alumni see the university as their personal fiefdom? How do some students manage to survive brutal academic climates, and what does it cost them? What can be done to change that? In *Black, Brown, Bruised: How Racialized STEM Education Stifles Innovation*, I ask these questions and analyze the answers. As with much research, asking one question leads to others. For instance, why do schools recruit people into disciplines whose climate regularly drives them away? It is inefficient, to say the least, for a university to train URM students only to have a large proportion of them leave without completing their degrees. What are the root causes of the lack of URM students and professionals in the STEM fields? What is the global community missing out on by tapping into only some of its human capital, namely, a small, male-dominated group that skews White and Asian? What contributions can Black, Latinx, and Indigenous peoples offer the STEM disciplines that no other groups of people can?

A DETAILED LOOK AT THE BOOK

In *Black, Brown, Bruised: How Racialized STEM Education Stifles Innovation*, I want you to hear the voices of scholars of color as they feel their way through a forbidding STEM educational landscape. Their moving personal accounts constitute a strong argument for doing everything possible to facilitate URMs' access to some of our society's most respected professions.

In chapter 1, I outline research that suggests the overrepresentation of White men in STEM has hampered scientific advancement and stifled innovation. There's a growing recognition that homogeneous work teams are significantly less effective at solving complex problems than teams that include people of varied classes, races, genders, and cultural backgrounds. In addition, researcher bias is more pronounced in teams made up of one demographic group. For instance, medical researchers often assume that men are the only subjects needed for drug trials, which leads to overdosing or ineffective treatment in nonmale groups. Car designers and engineers who test safety equipment with dummies the height and weight of an adult male run the risk of leaving people of all other sizes unprotected. Despite reams of evidence, the STEM enterprise continues to prop up its old-boy networks and exclude everyone else. It is an in-bred culture that refuses to acknowledge and be accountable for a recurring pattern of casual and blatant racial oppression.[3] Increasing racial diversity on STEM university campuses and in STEM industries would foster greater innovation, thereby leading to less racially insensitive environments and more effective STEM products and services. Embracing diversity in gender, sexual orientation, and types of ability, as well as neurodiversity (e.g., people with autism) and socioeconomic diversity, is not just a nice thing to add on to a campus culture or an R&D team; it could mean the difference between life and death.

Traditional STEM culture fosters the belief that the individual is the basic societal unit, and everyone has to make it on their own. It would be wiser to incorporate aspects of African, Latinx, and Indigenous cultures, which value group interests more than individuals, honor the wisdom of ancestral knowledge, and seek coexistence with nature rather than trying to conquer it. Other topics in chapter 1 include the Pan-Africanist perspective, LatCrit, and the dangerous pseudoscience of eugenics.

I also make an economic case for racial equity in STEM, which posits that, if the overall educational achievement of underrepresented students was raised to that of White students, the US economy would increase by $2.3 trillion by 2050, with STEM responsible for a large portion. Creating diverse and inclusive academic environments has been effective in reducing the STEM education gap. In addition, some current technologies, developed without URM participation, reinforce racial bias and discrimination. The benefits of diversifying STEM would accrue to all people, not just people of color (POC), and to the overall US economy.[4]

For several reasons, I start chapter 2 with a focus on engineering. I studied, trained, and worked as an engineer. It is a burgeoning field of study, in part because of the explosive growth of computers, computer science, and the related field of electrical engineering. Computers started as huge mainframes that occupied specially constructed rooms to keep them from overheating. Skilled operators, such as the Black women in the movie *Hidden Figures*, were needed just to keep them running, and programmers used punch cards. As microprocessors came into existence and became smaller and more efficient, computers gradually shrank while gaining capacity. Eventually, just about every office worker had a desktop computer, used for word processing, programming, spreadsheets, and other vital business tasks. Records kept on paper in filing cabinets gave way to records kept on hard drives. With the birth of the internet, followed by email and then social networking, computers cemented their place in our personal and work lives. Today, a smartphone can do far more than a mainframe computer ever could, and at speeds that mainframe designers could not dream of. For better or worse, we are constantly connected to our phones, tablets, laptops, and PCs, which hold vital information, entertainment, and all the personal connections of our lives and work. Naturally, electrical engineering and computing-related professions have also boomed.

Accordingly, engineering colleges and departments have expanded and hired faculty to accommodate those who want to enter these tech fields, but the peculiar institution of engineering has managed to create difficulties for eager POC who want to enter the field. Technology could be a great equalizer, but in many ways it has merely perpetuated social inequity. Engineering colleges and departments remain dominated by White men. Some Asian groups have made headway into the field as students and faculty, but otherwise these educational spaces have remained remarkably similar demographically to what they have been since engineering became a field of study.

The low participation rates of URMs in other STEM fields follow the pattern of engineering. Although biology, medicine, physics, and other STEM fields may lack the extreme POC-repelling qualities of engineering schools, the problems are rampant there, too. Racial stereotyping of URM groups as lacking intelligence and being limited in ability persists throughout most institutions of higher education, especially in technical, math-dependent fields, despite the presence of many URM graduates in these fields. It is hard to exaggerate the weight of constant disapproval of one's very being, and the denial of one's right to belong in a field of study, from people in authority who are paid to teach, train, and develop talent in students. It is also difficult to know how that disapproval feels unless one has experienced it personally. Racialized trauma and racial battle fatigue take a heavy toll on members of underrepresented groups who only want the same opportunities as their White and Asian peers. The resulting psychological and physical strain can wear down the brightest, most determined URM student and the most talented faculty member.

Using their words and stories, chapter 2 sketches a picture of life for URM students who seek to become STEM professionals, faculty members, researchers, and theorists. This chapter traces the struggles of students and faculty of color with the racist residue of STEM departments founded to serve White upper-class men. A particularly insidious form of racism is color blindness, or the attitude that it is rude to recognize a non-White person's race, ethnicity, or culture, as though it is something disgraceful. It works hand in glove with tokenism and the glut of research that trumpets resilience as the magic bullet for URM academic and career achievement. "Just withstand the racism that surrounds you, keep your nose to the grindstone, and you will succeed" is the unspoken message of color-blind resilience proponents.

Less-obvious forms of racism, such as structural and institutional racism, constitute the most impenetrable barrier to URMs thriving in STEM fields. Structural racism is the built-in kind, resting unseen at the foundations, often literally so, given that enslaved African Americans constructed the grand buildings of some of the country's oldest institutions of learning. Are a university's administrators, board members, department chairmen, faculty, and staff almost uniformly White? Structural racism. Do colleges founded to educate Black people have to sue to obtain the state funding they are owed, the same funding that flows freely to comparable historically White institutions (HWIs)? Are Black, Indigenous, and Latinx STEM workers paid less than White people doing the same job? Structural racism again.

Chapter 2 covers other factors that prevent the broad participation of URM students in STEM. Yet some students manage to vault all the obstacles of race and class and join the faculty, at which point they acquire unique burdens. For one, they are often presented as the university's answer to claims of racism. They are expected to almost singlehandedly solve the problem of lack of diversity at the institutions they serve, staffing committees on increasing diversity and mentoring every URM student who asks for it, on top of their teaching duties and research activities. Their contributions may be acknowledged, but they are not compensated or considered during evaluations. Often they willingly take on some of these extra commitments, which are not asked of White faculty, while still receiving only grudging acceptance at best from peers and students. Overtasked and still discriminated-against URM faculty members leave academia all too frequently, despite the appearance of having made it. Their departures represent the most tragic loss of all, given the decades they have spent preparing for those positions. When they do leave, the world loses the contributions to knowledge they would have added to the field through STEM innovation, research, teaching, and service. They also leave students of color without valuable role models, which helps to perpetuate the cycle of low URM participation in all STEM fields.

The voices of URM scholars also feature in chapters 3 through 5. Chapter 3 delves into the building blocks of racial discrimination. At the top of the list is racial stereotyping that demeans and devalues POC. Although stereotyping is hard to avoid, there is no upside to this human tendency to paint entire groups of people as either gifted or limited in their inherent abilities—and there is every reason to combat the tendency in oneself and others. I learned that stereotypes of Black and Asian students can be equally traumatizing, whether they are pigeonholed as naturally good at STEM subjects (Asians) or as the opposite (Blacks).[5] These stereotypes complicate education and career trajectories in STEM for both groups and cause significant psychological damage. It's almost impossible to avoid internalizing stereotypes, even when one is studying alone in a dorm room; the stereotypes accompany the students and cause internal havoc. It hurts to be stereotyped.

Some signs that people have been negatively affected by harmful stereotypes about themselves can manifest as impostor syndrome, going into survival mode, racial battle fatigue, and overworking to the point of sustaining physical and psychological harm. In their own self-defense, people on the receiving end of racial stereotypes adopt strategies and coping mechanisms to mitigate the resulting stress. Constantly working to exhaustion has predictable debilitating effects, but that doesn't keep URM students from doing just that. When URM STEM students are isolated—a typical condition in advanced classes in mathematics or another STEM discipline—and are unaware of the racialized structural barriers prevalent in STEM environments, they often begin to question if they or their racial group really are deficient. Feelings of being perceived as a failure can lead to hopelessness, and even if students persist in their STEM discipline, they do so with unnecessary and debilitating racialized stress. Learning to recognize racism and its effects serves as a racial buffer and helps students to differentiate and make sense of their racialized experiences.

Women of color in STEM spaces have to operate within the duality of being of color and a woman. This combines with the culture of most STEM departments, which were founded on and continue to value the knowledge of White men. Their teachers and advisers tend to favor people most like themselves. At best, they are unaware of the realities of these women's lives. At worst, they feel that women, especially URM women, have no business pursuing their chosen field. For all URM students, occupying structurally racist STEM environments can be demoralizing. Many URM students alter their dress and behavior in response to racist treatment, sometimes in efforts to camouflage their identities, other times to noisily declare their identification with their racial or ethnic group. The daily homework associated with implementing these coping mechanisms takes its own toll and uses up valuable energy.

A major defense against racialized assaults in STEM environments is the building of strong professional and personal identities. In chapter 3, I present case studies of highly educated Black STEM professionals who developed sophisticated ways of shielding themselves (but not fully) against racialized aggression in STEM environments. Their narratives trace the growth of their STEM identities from grade school through college and postgraduate education. They reveal how they dealt with race-based low expectations as youngsters and the wearying daily prejudice they still faced as degreed STEM professionals. Early responses to school-based racism included humiliation, fury, depression, and self-defeating behavior. However, they found sources of strength in such things as love of their subject, stereotype-challenging and stress-relieving humor, learning about their ancestral African culture, and joining supportive, culturally affirming organizations. I trace their progress from fragile identities to the robust STEM identities that have sustained them academically and professionally. Though they achieved their STEM academic goals, I want to stress that it was still not easy for them, and that nothing one person does can change an institution that is founded on and saturated with racism.

Many URM STEMers want to challenge social inequities through their work, which I call an equity ethic, described in chapter 4. The STEM arena loses many URM students to non-STEM disciplines not because they cannot do the work but because they see few opportunities to apply their expertise to problems they care about. Many of those problems arise from global racial inequities, in which the mass of non-White humanity often gets the short end of the stick. STEM professionals of color are generally less interested in maximizing profit for large corporations than in humanitarian goals, such as developing new drugs for malaria regardless of the profit-making potential. Their status as non-White Americans can also gain them greater access to people and countries in need of scientific and technical help. I argue that steering technical fields toward racial justice would be a powerful boon to retaining URM students in STEM fields and would lead to innovations that benefit people all over the world.

In contrast to some White students, URM students often demonstrate a social conscience. Many Black, Latinx, and Indigenous STEM students engage in mentoring and guiding younger students. They feel a communal responsibility to serve their neighborhoods, communities, and society at large, encouraging young people to dream beyond the limited futures they might feel bound by and to achieve in STEM to minister for a greater purpose. URM students' concerns might include their hometowns, people who resemble them phenotypically and often have shared values, or people they've never met whose suffering they cannot ignore. They want their work to help people lead better, healthier, and more equitable lives, and they often do not want to work for corporations that profit from war or that surveil their own communities. In their disciplines, however, any compassion they display can be viewed as weakness or a distraction from "true scientific" research, receiving no interest from professors and research advisers.

Attracting underrepresented students into STEM fields could very well depend on appealing to their equity ethic and making the learning environment more responsive to their unique and justice-oriented wants and needs. One pedagogical approach that has drawn numbers of Latinx students into engineering and related fields is community service learning, in which college students teach and mentor younger students with whom they share a culture. Another effective tactic is setting up learning communities characterized by collaboration and group work. Setting up secure environments and majority-women classes has also helped URM women students stay in their fields. In fact, anything that counters the individual-first tendency of STEM disciplines is especially inviting to both men and women of color.

The two final chapters examine current efforts that have increased URM participation in STEM fields and look at what needs to be done to further the trend. Chapter 5 covers race- and gender-conscious educational programs that position POC as being rich in knowledge and intellect. Also described are the principles underlying the most successful mentoring efforts for URMs. These programs tackle the racism and raced sexism in STEM academic spaces, but learning to cope with and respond to these barriers is not the goal; making STEM more inclusive of non-White people is. Effective educational approaches include

changing instructional methods and having faculty work to socialize
students into their disciplines by engaging them in research.

Many of these interventions have been shown to increase the comfort, satisfaction, and success of URM students in mathematical and
technical subject areas. Learning centers, financial support, and special
workshops in study skills and career exploration all have proven benefit, and so have academic advising and mentoring. It all starts with
understanding and seeking to improve the unique challenges that POC
endure in their STEM fields. Precollege summer programs that shep-
herd students from high school into college have helped a large majority of their participants earn degrees in the sciences and related fields. I
discuss some national and institutional mentoring efforts, such as the
Meyerhoff Scholars Program, the Minority Engineering Program, and
the Mathematics Workshop Program, as well as some basic principles
underlying effective URM student initiatives.

I also reveal the best mentoring practices for URM students in the
STEM disciplines, especially at the graduate level, where underrepresentation is even worse than among undergraduates. Having mentors who
share key identities (e.g., race, gender) has many benefits for mentees,
especially in terms of psychosocial support. However, the low number
of URM STEM faculty members means that few students of color get a
chance to see themselves in a faculty member like them or to receive
their support and guidance. Traditional mentoring programs rarely
consider how race is conceptualized, perceived, and enacted in STEM
learning and research environments. URM students therefore undergo
a taxing navigation process and have difficulty figuring out how to be
seen as valid contributor to the STEM knowledge-production. Thus,
despite some well-funded techniques and strategies that are most often
operationalized through mentoring, URMs still do not fully participate
in STEM.

It's abundantly clear that mentoring alone is not enough to counteract a university culture that reinforces racism. Mentoring programs can devolve into glorifications of personal resilience, once again leaving it up to individuals to soldier on despite resistance from authorities who do not want them to succeed. Chapter 6 offers practical guidance to STEM university administrators, industry leaders, and others on how to initiate fundamental change at their institutions. This includes suggestions for how to acknowledge and eliminate structural barriers facing URMs, thereby allowing these students to participate fully in the STEM enterprise. Drawing on my interviews with minority engineering program directors, university deans, and other administrators, I offer a multidimensional picture of how racism operates in the policies and practices of the STEM arena. I outline seven steps that academic leaders can take while working to dismantle discriminatory structural and racialized barriers. Setting up identity-conscious mentoring programs in STEM fields and employing more POC in STEM faculty positions are two critical steps. Candidates for these positions are available, and we need more than token representation among faculty in order to make a difference for URM students. Psychological counseling by URM professionals who understand the racialized trauma that URM students undergo is paramount. Current university counseling centers are understaffed, and counselors lack the expertise needed to make a difference for students who are subject to daily racialized assaults on campus. I also advocate creating avenues to business start-ups for POC and retraining STEM faculty in the rich cultures of Indigenous, Latinx, and Black people. It is also long past time to acknowledge the contributions of URM-serving institutions that have graduated a disproportionate number of students of color in STEM fields, in spite of being woefully underresourced, and to ensure that these institutions receive the funding they are owed.

The afterword contains my own story and career path to provide context for the many people I quote in this volume. In closing, I discuss the powerful vision of Afrofuturists, those far-seeing Black writers who have predicted scientific advances that have come to pass. They and I imagine a future in which POC thrive and make a difference. May that future arrive soon.

RACISM IN THE PANDEMIC

The virus that struck in the first quarter of 2020 has vividly illustrated some of this book's principles and concepts, so I close the introduction with a brief analysis of various aspects of the deadly Coronavirus, or COVID-19, in the population under study. Long before the virus arrived in the United States, Dr. David Williams, an internationally recognized social scientist who specializes in the study of social influences on health, stated the hard facts about Black death rates in myriad talks and publications. In 2017, Williams pointed out that approximately 220 Black people die unnecessarily every day, which means that every 6.5 minutes a Black person dies who likely would have survived if the health and health care of Black and White people were equal.[6] Williams, who is chair of the Department of Social and Behavioral Sciences at Harvard's T. H. Chan School of Public Health, argues that housing segregation is the most pernicious agent of racism in our country due to its deleterious effects on Black communities, including poor child nutrition, the stress of dealing with violence in everyday life, and poor access to good health care, all of which make Black Americans more likely to suffer from hypertension than Whites. Williams highlighted the fact that these disproportionate death rates apply equally to Black professionals and blue-collar workers. He and his colleagues have been calling attention to the negative effects racism has on Black people's health since 1990, but their evidence is nothing new; in 1899, W. E.

B. Du Bois exposed the higher rate of death from tuberculosis among Blacks as compared to Whites.[7]

Weathering, a health condition that leads to premature aging, is caused by the long-term physical, emotional, and psychological effects of racism, which severely challenge a person's ability to respond to their environment in a healthy manner.[8] So, for people of color, Blacks and Indigenous folk in particular, the impact of COVID-19 is nothing new. Weathering has been active in Black communities for centuries, masquerading as high rates of hypertension, heart disease, stroke, breast cancer, asthma, maternal morbidity, and other chronic conditions.[9] When David Williams and scholars like him hear reports that African Americans represent one-third of all deaths from COVID-19 in the United States although they represent only 13 percent of the population, I'm sure they are not surprised.[10]

President Trump's atrocious handling of the COVID-19 pandemic is a special kind of crazy, but its impact is similar to that of efforts by other White male leaders. When the vastly disproportionate number of deaths from COVID-19 among Blacks was finally reported, the mostly White, mostly male leadership set out to determine the reason for this racial disparity in death rates. However, these people are bona fide members of the neoliberal system of monopoly-finance capital that puts profits before people, including lower-income Whites, and the planet.[11] Grocery clerks, delivery truck drivers, cleaning staff, and many other blue-collar workers are now being identified as essential while at the same time being positioned as disposable, in that continuing to work puts them at greater risk of contracting COVID-19.[12]

In some cities, Blacks are dying of COVID-19 at six times the rate of Whites.[13] Many people of color have dire health conditions that make them more vulnerable to the virus, including diabetes and heart disease, which are largely the result of a socioeconomic system that degrades the quality of their lives and deprives them of affordable health care. Fabiola Cineas, senior editor at *Philadelphia Magazine*, put it succinctly: "Hundreds of years of racism has delivered poor health and economic outcomes for black people, making them more vulnerable in the pandemic."[14] Six Black women scholars who specialize in epidemiology, community health sciences, biostatistics, and urban health argued that using frameworks such as critical race theory can further reveal the conditions that make Blacks particularly vulnerable to COVID-19 and other inequities in health-care outcomes by focusing on the structural role residential racial segregation plays in mass incarceration and heavy policing of Black neighborhoods.[15] Dr. Kizzmekia Corbett, a Black Meyerhoff Scholars alum (see chapter 5 for details on this academic mentoring program) and a viral immunologist at the Vaccine Research Center at the National Institute of Allergy and Infectious Diseases, is leading the team of scientists working on a coronavirus vaccine.[16] The race to develop a vaccine is a race against death, in particular among Black people, whom some in the Trump administration are essentially blaming for their own deaths. For example, US Surgeon General Jerome Adams made much-publicized remarks that the Black community should avoid use of "drugs, tobacco, and alcohol" during the pandemic and to do it for their "big momma," thereby demonstrating his unwillingness to see racism as the cause of disproportionate Black death rates.[17]

Centuries of data demonstrate that most Black folks do not have the same opportunity as most Whites to live healthy lives.[18] The Trump administration and many governors put saving the economy ahead of protecting lives, which reflects an inhumane socioeconomic system that disproportionately hurts the most marginalized.[19] Science for the People, a progressive organization devoted to social change, has tackled such STEM biases as the militarization of scientific research, corporate control of research agendas, the environmental consequences of energy policy, and health-care inequality. On March 20, 2020, the organization delivered a statement on COVID-19 demanding "that any science and technology developed to respond to the pandemic [be made] available for all, without profit or patent" to ensure a peaceful global response to the pandemic.[20] So, what does this have to do with the plight of the unrepresented and racially minoritized working in STEM fields?

Over the past century, the amount of time and money invested in science has vastly increased, but a per-dollar or per-person evaluation suggests that science is becoming far less efficient and productive.[21] Despite vast increases in the time and money spent on STEM research, current progress is not keeping pace with that of the past. I argue that a lack of diversity plays a key role in this stagnation of STEM. The field has invested heavily in new products that reflect a predominantly White focus, an unwillingness to reckon with the possibility that racism actually underpins research, and a lack of contextualization for the deep and problematic history of race and racism in science.[22] For instance, the co-inventor of the transistor, William Shockley, was an unremorseful racist and a supporter of eugenics. Carl Linnaeus, the father of biological taxonomy and originator of the system of species and the term *homo sapiens*, was also a central figure in the emergence of scientific racism.[23] If all people in all racial groups were nurtured in the STEM arena the way most White men are nurtured, would COVID-19 be devastating the global population, especially the most vulnerable, the way it is today?

CHAPTER ONE

Will White Supremacy
End America's STEM Supremacy?

The Costs of Excluding People of Color
from STEM Education

WHEN I WAS A LITTLE GIRL, I used to watch *The Jetsons*, a cartoon produced by Hanna-Barbera. If you were born in the 1950s through the
1970s, you may recall the introduction in which the Jetsons and their
fellow neighbors fly around in their mini-spaceship cars. And it's funny
that when I watched *The Jetsons*, I didn't really pay attention to the
fact that everyone in it was White.[1] Nor did I fuss about the patriarchal roles that deprived women and girls of their full humanity. The
prescribed roles for their children did not faze me. I only saw the flying
mini-spaceship cars and other technological novelties, which helped
me envision a future where I'd be flying in my car. I was 100 percent
confident that by the time I became a full-fledged, out-of-college adult
with my own crib, not only would I possess a purple-and-brown flying
car, but the streets and highways would be full of bikes, roller skates,
and skateboards because everybody in a vehicle would be up in the air.
Even today, I believe that we actually should be flying in our cars and
having a whole lot more in the way of sophisticated technologies that
improve our lives and do not damage the planet.

So, what happened? I blame the individualistic, ultracompetitive,
overwhelmingly White (with some tokenized Asians), mostly heterosexual, militaristically grounded, middle- to upper-class, nationalist,

19

able-bodied, biased STEM culture. This is the very STEM culture that has not invented flying cars and has delayed or halted other seemingly out-of-this-world innovations. I didn't think my childhood dreams were naive, but I didn't yet understand the power of racism or how racism and other forms of discrimination would ultimately hold us back from being collectively creative and producing STEM products and services beyond our wildest individual dreams. If you take this journey with me, you will begin to realize that you too should be flying in your car. Said differently, racism and discrimination hamper STEM and STEMers' abilities to be as ingenious and imaginative as they can be, thereby stifling innovation in these fields.

Forces such as rapid changes in technology, changing racial and ethnic demographics, national security, and globalization have also fueled the need to increase and diversify the computing and engineering workforce at colleges and universities, but exploring these factors is beyond the scope of this book. The principles and values of the cultural founders of STEM are fueling the current focus on beating China, building more nuclear bombs, stealing and selling personal information, and, in the process, killing our Earth. These values produce technological advances that don't improve or enhance the human condition. However, when I envisioned an advanced scientific and technological, antiracist, dream world as a young Black girl growing up on Chicago's South Side, I did not predict that we could draw on the vast variety of the human diaspora and incorporate the social sciences, education, anthropology, ethnic studies, and cultural studies into designing and creating for all humanity. Today I see that vision as eminently achievable and desirable.

When I tell audiences about how I saw my future, I am frequently dismissed because I can't definitively prove that if we had more racial diversity in the STEM arena, along with neurodiversity and gender, sexual orientation, and socioeconomic diversity, flying cars would not seem so far-fetched. There is always someone in the audience who tells me about the ten billionaires who actually do have flying cars. But I'm not talking about them folk. I'm talking about me and you and our neighbors in flying cars, like right now.

THIS PROBLEM IS GREATER AND GRAVER
THAN SKIN DEEP

Currently, *66 percent of US science and engineering professionals are White or Asian men; if White and Asian women are included, the number is 88 percent.*[2] STEM fields have influenced nearly every aspect of human life, so the ability to cultivate talent in the STEM arena links directly to our everyday lives. Researchers have found that when a team tries to solve difficult problems, *the diversity of the problem solvers matters more than their individual ability.*[3] Breakthroughs in complex problems often result from bringing together diverse perspectives, backgrounds, ideologies, and reflections. Being able to see a problem differently from others on the team is often critical to a breakthrough, and thus *diversity is integral to the effectiveness of a work team.* The goal of STEM should therefore be to lessen and ultimately eliminate opportunity differentials that limit the human potential and the STEM contributions of underrepresented people of color. Being marginalized by race in this society gives a person a trove of painfully acquired knowledge. That knowledge makes it possible to ask a whole different set of questions and encourages innovative and racially conscious approaches.

Psychology professors Douglas Medin and Carol Lee believe that researcher bias skews results. According to them, scientific validity "involves choices about what problems to study, what populations to study, and what procedures and measures should be used. In making these choices, diverse perspectives and values are important."[4] When White middle-class scientists conduct research on a mostly White middle-class population, for example, their results based on this limited sample often do not apply to other demographic sectors, which differ from one another physically, socially, and culturally. Medin and Lee also point out that "evidence of the fundamental role of culture in human learning suggest[s] that there is no reason to think learning in science or the practices of science is somehow acultural or simplistically universal."[5]

I believe that rugged individualism may have run its course as the premier value in Western society; it is time to invite the wisdom of other cultures, often devalued ones, into learning at all levels of US education. One school of thought, Afrocentricity, counters the highly valued Eurocentric traits of competition and individualism with the cooperation, harmony, and collaboration that generally underlie African cultures. Ghanaian native George Sefa Dei sees Afrocentricity as being about inclusion, about "opening up a new and transformed consciousness for all peoples."[6] In his vision of Afrocentric schooling, a classroom that communicates "the values of human coexistence with one another and with nature (not control over nature), group solidarity, mutuality, collective work, and responsibility" allows students to perceive group interests as taking priority over their individual interests.[7] This understanding contrasts starkly with the Western belief that personal success is solely the result of individual striving, often at the expense of other people. Another African educator, Peggy Gabo Ntseane, articulates a way of thinking that her country nurtures: "In the Botswana cultural context, where we believe that *motho ke motho ka batho ba bagwe* (i.e., there is no self without the collective), it makes sense to look at the role of support from other individuals, family, community, and overall cultural values in the process of transformational learning."[8]

Indigenous and Latinx people are the other two major groups included under the umbrella term "underrepresented and racialized minorities" (URMs), who are the focus of this book.[9] Their educational traditions are also worth exploring. Indigenous researchers say that Indigenous students "need a firm grounding in the accumulated wisdom of our ancestors" in order to be prepared to solve future problems.[10] This entails authentic honoring of the mathematical contributions of Indigenous students' communities.[11] Bev Caswell and colleagues invoke a concept learned from Ojibwe elders, *gaa-maamiwi-asigaginendamowin*, an Anishnaabemowin word that translates roughly as "gathering to learn and do mathematics together, collectively performing useful action."[12] Furthermore, TribalCrit contends that settler colonialism operates similarly to racism but has important distinctions that account for the unique ways settler colonialism has affected Indigenous peoples.[13]

Latinx encompasses a range of Latin American nationalities with varied political histories. For Mexicans and Puerto Ricans, two of the largest Latinx groups, US educational practices and policies have ensured their marginalization through "limited access to separate, inferior, subtractive and non-academic instruction."[14] Funds of Knowledge, a concept derived from Luis Moll and Norma Gonzalez, is an antideficit framework that unearths and leverages knowledge produced in the cultural-historical experiences of Latinx students' families and communities.[15] Funds of Knowledge has demonstrated that Latinx families and communities have robust bodies of knowledge and skills essential for communal functioning and well-being.[16]

Together, these three groups embody a *pedagogy of solidarity* that "hinges on radical differences and that insists on relationships of incommensurable interdependency."[17] In STEM education, Black-, Latinx-, and Indigenous-led scholarship and the coming together of their respective communities to combat White supremacy have created an organization that brings together scholars of color in mathematics education to leverage our individual and collective expertise in mathematics education; voice our ideas and concerns related to the field; conceptualize and locate ourselves in anti-oppressive and humane mathematics education agendas; and share self-care and leadership strategies to sustain and nourish ourselves in this justice struggle. [18]

Black, Brown, Bruised: How Racialized STEM Education Stifles Innovation, although centered more on the Black STEM experience, calls for increased solidarity across URM groups in STEM education to illuminate new ways of nourishing and affirming Indigenous, Latinx, and Black students' racial and STEM identities along with our individual and shared cultural strengths.[19]

SCIENTISTS AGREE THAT MORE DIVERSITY IS NEEDED

"White men make up less than 50 percent of the U.S. population. We're drawing [future scientists] from less than 50 percent of the talent we have available," said Dr. Mae Jemison, the first Black woman astronaut, who has a medical degree and a bachelor's in chemical engineering and African and African American studies. "The more people you have in STEM," she said, "the more innovations you'll get."[20]

The National Institutes of Health director, Francis Collins, has said that chronic underrepresentation in the workforce leads to "the inescapable conclusion that we are missing critical contributors to our talent pool."[21] Considering that most children born in the United States are non-White and that we fill most of our graduate STEM programs with international students, there should be crisis-level concern about the need to cultivate domestic talent of color in STEM. Diversity in terms of gender is another important consideration. The National Center for Women & Information Technology compared the number of patents filed by mixed-sex teams and all-male teams and found that the mixed-sex teams filed over 40 percent more patents than the all-male teams.[22] A more diverse STEM population portends huge benefits to scientific and technological innovation. An editorial entitled "Science Benefits from Diversity" in Nature, a prominent scientific journal, also argues that improving the participation of URM people is not only the right thing to do, it actually would lead to better research.[23]

Facebook and other STEM companies have argued that their diversity problem is due to a leaky tech pipeline, in which racially marginalized students are not gaining the required education needed to be appropriately represented in technology positions.[24] However, some argue that there is no technology pipeline problem for Black students since there are currently twice as many Black graduates with computer science degrees as there are hires from this group.[25] My colleague Dr. Lou Matthews, former minister of education in Bermuda, argued that the pipeline argument is an insult to pipelines, which flow with much less dysfunction and less bias than this passive metaphor claims.[26] Solutions presented to fix the leaks in the STEM pipeline focus on fixing the student while leaving the institution and the key stakeholders untouched. Moreover, these efforts do not challenge the pipeline as an anti-inclusive design of STEM education and the participation that is at its core as structurally racist. So, what does contribute to the inequities in STEM education and employment? Tech investor and Black entrepreneur Katherine Finney said, "What they [Silicon Valley companies] are really saying is, there aren't enough Black and Hispanic graduates who fit in."[27] To combat the issue of hiring bias in the tech industry, Black engineer Stephanie Lampkin created a blind job-match application that she hopes will help keep companies accountable through the use of data and provide a fair pathway to technology jobs for innovators of color.[28] (Note that a Black woman rather than a White man came up with this equitable software solution.)

URMs are not the only people who object to workplaces that do not reflect US demographics. Eight in ten Americans who responded to a Pew Research Center survey in 2017 said ethnically and racially diversified workplaces are important to them, and 45 percent said diverse perspectives are critical to organizational success.[29] However, Blacks working in STEM are about four times as likely as Whites in STEM to say their workplace doesn't pay enough attention to increasing racial and ethnic diversity and are particularly likely to say they have experienced workplace discrimination because of their race.[30]

Enabling the full creative and economic potential of the STEMers who have been traditionally stigmatized will be critical to sustaining STEM innovation and achieving an equitable STEM vision for the future. It also makes good financial sense to have more people of color gainfully employed. For example, a 2018 report by the Kellogg Foundation on the economic outlook for Michigan projected that closing the racial equity gap by educating and employing URMs to their fullest potential in the next thirty years would increase the state's economic output by $92 billion.[31] These gains would derive largely from higher earnings for currently underemployed groups, increased consumer spending and tax revenues from these groups, and decreased spending on social services and health-related costs.

Being White in America comes with the benefit of being part of a culture that is portrayed as normative and ideal, one that other cultures should try to emulate. Notions of Whiteness have defined both Whites and people of color in this society, while color blindness serves to diminish or attempts to negate the realities of this systemically biased structure.[32] Non-Whiteness is almost always compared to Whiteness as the norm, and difference is therefore mostly positioned as inferior. This paradigm goes largely unquestioned, a by-product of a racialized societal system in which educational, economic, political, social, and ideological levels are largely structured to shape the life chances of different racial groups.[33] White privilege does have a class- and pedigree-based hierarchy, but all Whites in America benefit from unmerited privilege. They also write the script for what is valued in America: respect for competition, universalism, nuclear family structure, time being perceived as finite, and rugged individualism—otherwise known as meritocracy. URM students struggle to develop and deploy coping mechanisms to safeguard their academic survival and to counter negative evaluations in toxic educational environments.

The question before us: Should we ask URM students to become grittier and more resilient, or should our society as a whole be more committed to disarming the structures of racism so that URM students do not have to be resilient to the point that they compromise their mental and physical well-being?[34] A related question: What are the short-term and long-term effects of continually attempting to achieve in an environment where encountering a steady flow of race and gender obstacles is the accepted norm? We should contemplate how much grit and perseverance are healthy and nurturing. How much longer, and at what cost, do URM learners have to continue working to exhaustion and still not get the credit they deserve?

URM INTELLECTUAL STEM THOUGHT: THEY'VE BEEN THERE ALL ALONG

> One could not be a calm, cool, and detached scientist
> while Negroes were lynched, murdered, and starved.
> —W. E. B. Du Bois, 1899

From the late 1800s through the 1930s—and continuing through a present-day revival of eugenics—White psychologists, sociologists, and statisticians embraced concepts of White supremacy to prove their racial superiority through "science." Prominent Black intellectual W. E. B. Du Bois ardently disputed the idea that Blacks could be scientifically proven to be inferior.[35] We do not often think of Dr. Du Bois as a warrior in the fight for STEM racial inclusion, but his unrelenting challenge to scientific racism puts him at the foundation of Black intellectual thought in STEM.[36]

Diverse scholars produce research focused on developing and articulating URM intellectual thought in STEM. URM scholars who are concerned with racial justice in STEM have long said that the need to consider the broader social and structural constraints that foster racial underrepresentation in diverse STEM fields impede URM progress, representation, and achievement in STEM. In the STEM arena, URM intellectuals are scholars and activists who critique the mainstream discourse and treatment of URM people in STEM, with the purpose of transforming their conditions while improving the totality of the larger STEM community. In particular, Jomo Mutegi operates from a Pan-Africanist perspective, with an understanding that the life conditions of African Americans are essentially the same as the life conditions of people of African descent globally.[37] From his Pan-Africanist perspective, he argues that the salience of African American underrepresentation in STEM disciplines is connected to the global systemic racism that afflicts all people of African descent. His work has advanced important research on the ways that systemic racism shapes the African STEM workforce beyond unequal representation, given that his questions and insights are germane to African people broadly. L. R. Thompson, J. L. Davis, and Jomo Mutegi argue for centering the social conditions of Black people as a driving purpose for their STEM education while critically assessing the pedagogy and curriculum of African people.[38] Their interviews with Black STEM researchers and educators have provided invaluable insights about the importance of Black STEM intellectual thought, including increasing the level of African American contributions to the technological advancement of this country, fostering critical thinking among African Americans as a means to create social change, and a "liberatory agenda" that has the goal of building and improving "the status of Black people globally." Their model of a socially transformative curriculum argues that students of African descent must engage in critical discourse about their social conditions and use their scientific knowledge to change those conditions.

Latinx STEM researchers have posited that Latinx STEM students will have greater and more holistic success when they have cultural congruity with their discipline.[39] Recent work of Latinx thought leaders in STEM concludes that the language used in engineering recruitment needs to be more directly aimed toward Latinxs by involving community leaders and using creative techniques to engage parents and even grandparents, who are often instrumental in familial decision making at the household level. Such "crosswalks" between family, community, and higher education, otherwise known as community service learning (CSL), are particularly important for Latinx STEM engagement.[40] Given that many Hispanic-serving institutions (HSIs) are located in or near communities with large Latinx populations, CSL has been particularly beneficial for Latinx students by providing a greater sense of belonging and contributing to their communities.[41] Thus, STEM research and innovation from this community of URM STEM scholars include Latinx intellectual tradition by presenting the reality of racialized life and experiences in STEM from the point of view of URM people learning and participating in STEM themselves.[42] STEM researchers also employ Latinx critical theory (LatCrit) and community cultural wealth frameworks to analyze and understand the experiences of Latinx STEM students and faculty.[43] LatCrit seeks better understanding of the full breadth of racialization, which includes analysis of how ethnicity, language, and national origin converge to "otherize" and politically disenfranchise Latinx people in the United States.[44] LatCrit has been used to investigate the intersection of identities in Latinx students and faculty, including immigration status, ethnicity, language, sexuality, phenotype, accent, and surname, and to question the standards of the dominant culture.[45]

Indigenous scholars overwhelmingly conclude that students who adapt to campus life while maintaining their culture are more likely to succeed in academia than are Indigenous students who adopt assimilationist strategies.[46] Indigenous STEM thought leaders rely on integrating cultural aspects into a science learning environment to provide strong support to Native students for their self-efficacy in science and identity as scientists.[47] Through acknowledgment of language and culture, tribal colleges and universities (TCUs) provide a support system for students. In addition to Indigenous science, TCUs also offer STEM-related courses and research opportunities. Many of these aspects help Native students to be more engaged in their academic programs.[48] Indigenous scholars in STEM also harbor a fear that Indigenous students' engagement with Western science may lead to the loss of traditional values.[49]

A NOTE ON RESEARCH METHODOLOGIES

This book draws on research I began in 2009. I often use a phenomenological approach, which is appropriate when the goal is to explore the perspectives of research participants. Phenomenological qualitative research relies heavily on in-depth interviews for data collection; it is particularly useful for investigating insider perspectives. The goal of a phenomenological approach is to develop a composite description of how people experience a particular phenomenon. I have also employed multiple case study analysis, which is useful for understanding complex social phenomena, such as those surrounding how racism and sexism manifest in students' STEM contexts and how students respond to them.

I have generally gained access to study participants through (1) a convenience sample of existing professional connections, (2) face-to-face recruiting at national conferences, and (3) systematic sampling of institutions (e.g., those with five or more tenured or tenure-track Black engineering faculty). I invited potential participants to take part in the study, which consisted of video- or audio-recorded interviews (with permission) or focus groups for all participants and an additional survey for subgroups; other studies involved private audio- or video-recorded interviews lasting an hour or more. I drew from a diverse array of institutions, including historically White institutions (HWIs), historically Black colleges and universities (HBCUs), Hispanic serving institutions (HSIs), private universities, public institutions, and technological institutes. Selecting many types of institutions was valuable because their varying social contexts reflect different pressures, supports, and resources affecting the participants.

JOURNEY THROUGH STEM WITH STEMERS OF COLOR

Take this journey with me, as we examine the consequences of being in a discipline where societal beliefs persist about the incompetence and cultural inability of URMs to achieve in STEM. I will unpack the persistent obligation and burden of URMs to prove themselves over and over and over again, often creating extra forms of stress and strain. This examination will include the structures within STEM higher education that perpetually exclude URM students. I am hoping to convince you that dismantling or at least chipping away at structurally biased barriers in STEM can lead to offering URMs the experience of full membership in STEM that has the potential to alter our technological future, including flying in our cars.

CHAPTER TWO

The Plight of the Underrepresented in STEM Higher Education and the Workforce

MAURICE WAS A BRIGHT CHICAGO-AREA HIGH SCHOOL STUDENT with a strong interest in engineering and the math and science chops to back it up.[1] Popular with teachers and fellow students, Maurice also prided himself on his code-switching skills: his ability to move seamlessly from Black vernacular to formal English. During a summer internship as an engineer in training, however, he discovered the reality of being Black in a civil engineering company:

> The [South Asian] Indian and some of the White engineers in my group section rarely spoke to me, unless my manager was around. Then they [the engineers] treated me extra nice, which disgusted me even more. Most of the engineers hate the managers too. All the managers are White males, except for one White lady. Now you would think that we would get along because they treat her kinda like they treat me [invisible], but she treats me like I'm a nuisance. The White managers treat me like an affirmative action, token Negro: all they talk about is my potential. I could design a bridge system that could save the company a hundred thousand dollars and they would still be talking about my potential.

In other words, Maurice wasn't out of high school before he learned that all his intellect, knowledge, hard work, and assimilation skills had gotten him to a place where he could hardly stand to be. It was eating away at his desire to embark on the career he used to want:

> I just don't like [engineering] enough to put up with the BS . . . Now, if I went into civil engineering and I got my PhD—let's say I even got two PhDs—every day, someone somewhere is going to question and challenge my ability to do my job. Sometimes it will be subtle, other times it will be in my face, but it will always be there. That I know.

The tokenism, isolation, underestimation, and other signs of entrenched, silent racism that Maurice encountered are standard operating procedure in workplaces designed and controlled by upper-class White men. What's unusual about Maurice is that he found out so young exactly how working in such a place would feel. In this chapter, I describe URMs' struggles with racism through the highest levels of higher education. I also outline institutional and structural barriers that impede the broad participation of students of color in STEM. The chapter closes with a discussion of unique problems facing URM STEM faculty members and researchers, who leave their jobs at the highest rates of all racial and ethnic groups.

SPOTLIGHT ON ENGINEERING:
JUST HOW UNDERREPRESENTED ARE URMS?

Engineering provides an extreme example of URM underrepresentation in STEM, but the difference from other STEM fields is only one of degree. In recent years, increasing numbers of students have chosen engineering majors, and more professors were hired to teach them— 12.5 percent more over the decade since 2009. URM groups have not been included in the increase, however. Nationwide, Asian American engineering faculty grew from 22.7 to 28.3 percent of the total, Latinxs went from 3.5 to 3.8 percent, and the percentage of Pacific Islander

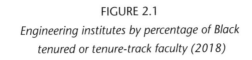

FIGURE 2.1

*Engineering institutes by percentage of Black
tenured or tenure-track faculty (2018)*

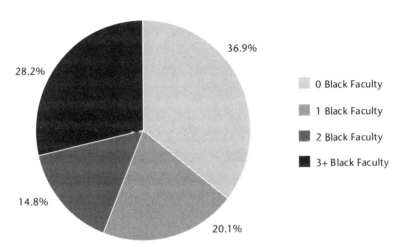

Source: Joseph Roy, "Profile by Engineering and Engineering Technology Colleges," *Profile by Engineering and Engineering Technology Colleges,* 2018 ed. (Washington, DC: American Society for Engineering Education, 2019).

and Black engineering faculty edged up fractionally. During a decade of growth, Black engineering faculty remained between 2 and 3 percent of the total (2.4 percent as of 2019) despite various programs aimed at broadening the participation of URMs in engineering (see figure 2.1).[2] Of almost three hundred engineering schools surveyed, 36.9 percent had *no* African American faculty and only 28.2 percent had at least three African American faculty members. Table 2.1 compares the ethnic and gender breakdown of engineering faculty from 2008 to 2018.[3]

Even at HBCUs, the composition of STEM faculty also shows disparities along race, ethnicity, and gender lines. In 2014, 53 percent of full professors in HBCU STEM departments were White men, 43 percent

TABLE 2.1

Percentage of engineering faculty by ethnicity and gender: 27,412 (2018)

	2008	*2018*	*% Change*
Women	12.3	17.6	43.1
Asian Americans	22.7	28.3	32.9
Latinx Americans	3.5	3.8	15.6
African Americans	2.5	2.4	4.0
Hawaiians/Pacific Islanders	0.1	0.1	0.0
Institutions with at least 5% African American faculty members	12.6	10.7	15.1

Source: Joseph Roy, "Engineering by Numbers." *Engineering by Numbers,* 2018 ed. (Washington, DC: American Society for Engineering Education, 2019), https://www.asee.org/documents/papers-and-publications/publications/college-profiles/2018-Engineering-by-Numbers-Engineering-Statistics-UPDATED-15-July-2019.pdf.

were Hispanic, and just 28 percent were African American men.[4] The proportion of female STEM faculty at HBCUs had not increased much since 2001, when it was 38.7 percent.[5]

In addition, while the total number of US doctoral engineering degrees awarded grew almost 34 percent from 2010 to 2018, foreign nationals earned more than half these degrees. African Americans continue to earn the lowest share of PhDs in engineering; more than half the 203 engineering schools that responded to a national survey awarded *no* doctoral degrees to Black students.[6] From 2009 to 2016, the numbers of African American graduate students in engineering actually decreased.[7] After graduation, White PhDs dominate full-time positions at research-intensive universities, while their Black counterparts hold less than 5 percent of these jobs.[8] White men also dominate computer science doctoral programs: from 2004 to 2016, White men earned more computer science PhDs than all other groups combined.[9]

MAJOR BARRIERS TO THE BROAD PARTICIPATION
OF URM STUDENTS IN STEM

Students of color are discouraged by the low numbers of URM people in technical and scientific fields and the associated lack of support from a network or from URM faculty. Many are reluctant to become the only person of color or one of few in their fields. Education researcher Beth Baker looked at causes of the scarcity of URMs in biological sciences and found a cyclical pattern in which a lack of URMs in teaching positions leads to a lack of URM students, which results in fewer replacement URM biology teachers and professionals, and so on. For instance, of 4,321 doctoral degrees awarded in biological sciences in 1995, 105 went to African Americans, 126 went to Hispanics, and 15 to Indigenous people.[10]

Research on this subject is confirmed by the several hundred URM professionals I have encountered who speak with great agony about the various ways they were pushed out of STEM or suffer while remaining in these fields. Most cite one or more of the following reasons for leaving or loathing their chosen STEM fields or careers:

• Demeaning racial stereotypes from STEM faculty that place them at the bottom of a racialized STEM hierarchy, which puts international Asians at the top, followed by international Europeans, Whites, and other international students, and then by Latinx, Black, and Indigenous people.
• Too few URM (or racially minoritized) students and faculty in the STEM disciplines.
• URM students' difficulty envisioning themselves as part of the STEM workforce in the face of racially charged STEM academic environments.
• Lack of opportunities to pursue work related to racial justice and activism in their current STEM environments.

- Unwelcoming institutional climates and the revolving-door syndrome of URM faculty, who leave their institutions and sometimes leave academia because a PhD in STEM—even one from a prestigious STEM university—does not save professors of color from racial battle fatigue.

The concept of *racial battle fatigue*, brought to prominence by education scholar William A. Smith and his colleagues, maintains that race-related stressors (e.g., the differential exposure to on-campus racism and discrimination and the time and energy that stereotyping demands from Black students) can cause debilitating psychological and physiological stress.[11] Feelings of powerlessness, invisibility, loss of integrity, or pressure to represent one's group often accompany racialized stress in these environments.[12] The psychological and behavioral responses to race-related stressors include anger, escapism, withdrawal, frustration, and avoidance and are consistent with the notion of racial battle fatigue as a psychological response to racism and discrimination.

In a study colleagues and I performed, "'I Know I Have to Work Twice as Hard and Hope That Makes Me Good Enough': Exploring the Stress and Strain of Black Doctoral Students in Engineering and Computing," we used the theory of racial battle fatigue to identify how these advanced students' racialized experiences were being operationalized.[13] Racial battle fatigue was evident in the students' responses to trauma and the experience of stress symptoms, as the participants gave up on thriving in the doctoral programs and simply aimed to stay alive and complete their degrees. Thus, we added survival mode to the other psychological responses that occur in racial battle fatigue. *Survival mode* manifests as a signal to the body and brain that well-being may be at risk, and the common response is to ignore or greatly compromise one's self-care. Survival mode includes students triggering a toxic mentality to continually push through negative encounters (often racialized experiences) that cause significant distress in order to persist in their programs. Survival mode directs almost all a person's energy to simply holding on for dear life.

THE BURDENS OF TOKENISM, COLOR BLINDNESS, AND RESILIENCE

Maya had recently earned a doctorate in mechanical engineering from a public Southern HWI. She was one of a group of HBCU students who had entered the sister institution's engineering department as part of a special program. According to Maya and other students in her group, the HWI faculty members patronized the Black students from the program, and some White students called them "monkeys." In this racially charged atmosphere, Maya felt obliged to display a persona that countered stereotypes:

> The only Black interaction that they'll have is me. I might be the only person in the department. Especially . . . international students; they may not have met any Black person ever, so it's me. So it's kind of like I have to be a representative for the race and I can't come off certain ways because I don't want to turn them off [and make them think], "Well, Black people act this way. Black women act this way," especially with the angry Black woman stereotype. It sometimes makes me so upset, but I can't get angry even though, shit, I'm well within my right to get angry. I don't want to feed into the, the perceptions that they may have.

Maya had a caring White adviser who "went the extra mile" to support her academically, but he dropped the ball when she brought up the stress caused by being the only woman of color in the lab. He said, "Just be the person you need to be and don't worry about the color of your skin and your sex. Just worry about the engineering."

Maya's adviser was demonstrating the belief known as color blindness, as in the liberal trope "I don't see color; I just see people."
Color-blind ideology presents an unrealistic demand to pretend that
racism does not exist or is not important.[14] This attitude is sometimes
deployed in the hope that it will defeat the power of racism.[15] Sadly,
color-blind ideology requires URM students to discount the reality of
their experiences and emotions and lets racism continue unchallenged
(because one cannot challenge something that does not exist). Also,
color blindness implies that if race is not an important difference, the
lack of people of color in a given field therefore means that they are
uninterested in the subject, have no talent for it, or do not put in the
necessary effort.[16]

Telling Maya not to worry about her color also implies that her skin
color and gender are problematic. In other words, if she could only
pretend she was no different from the people in the dominant White
group, Maya could blend into the departmental culture and all would
be well. That clearly was not going to happen in the virulently racist climate of Maya's engineering department. Those who insulted and
demeaned the Black students felt safe doing so because the department
and the institution did nothing to stop it; their attitudes and their inac-
tion had implicit institutional support. Thus, it is not surprising that a
well-meaning mentor and toxic levels of prejudice could coexist.

An institutional mission statement that advocates inclusive behavior does not guarantee that minoritized students will be accepted every-
where they go on campus—or anywhere on campus, for that matter—as
URM students and faculty are well aware. Institutional bias means that
even apparently positive traditions and practices favor some groups
and disadvantage others. Many HWIs have benefited from the labor of
enslaved Africans during their founding days, so it could be said that
oppression of particular racial groups is an unacknowledged core value.
National research-funding agencies reproduce these inequities through

their practices.[17] URM STEM faculty experience the discrimination and stress of having their research devalued and being out of the loop about strategies to advance their careers.[18] In addition, when Black faculty are expected to speak for others who share their racial identity, it can produce anxiety via performance pressure.[19] Those who are tokenized can feel a heightened sense of having to be constantly on point, as Maya reported; any errors they make are magnified because they are seen as reflecting on an entire racial group rather than the individual.[20] Innovation requires trying out new ideas publicly, so the normal risks associated with being a STEM student can create additional stress for URM students. They often feel they cannot afford to innovate without being negatively stereotyped, which could harm other URM students and faculty when their individual mistakes are identified as ability-related failures tied to their race.

THE INTERPLAY OF COLOR BLINDNESS, RESILIENCE, AND STRUCTURAL AND INSTITUTIONAL RACISM

Research and practice efforts have concentrated on changing URMs to fit into dominant perspectives, such as color-blindness, neoliberalism and individual resilience, despite a lack of support systems. In 2018, education researcher Kevin Clay reported on a phenomenon he called Black resilience neoliberalism in a group of Black students enrolled in an Upward Bound precollege program. In this belief system, the power of entrenched racist structures is accepted and discounted and Black people are solely responsible for overcoming social inequities.[21] Black resilience neoliberalism accepts structural racism as a given and normalizes the act of enduring or strategically overcoming it. Some of Clay's student participants blamed poor Black people for their own problems, calling out supposed extravagances as the cause of their poverty. The resilience mantra is also present in "empowerment" and "grit" rhetoric

that celebrates exceptional Black people, such as Barack Obama and
Oprah Winfrey, and asserts that anyone can make it if they try hard
enough.[22]

Color blindness and resilience ideology work hand in hand with
structural racism, which is a complex of social relations that shapes
the life chances of various racial groups by producing systemic racial
advantages for the dominant racial group and disadvantages for subor-
dinate races.[23] According to Eduardo Bonilla-Silva and David Dietrich,
color-blind racism is an institutionalized system that minimizes the
force of racism, making it possible for some people to claim that we live
in a postracial world.[24] Color-blind beliefs urge disadvantaged people
to become resilient, while social, political, and educational systems
continue to abuse and neglect them.[25] These ideologies enable racism
to go unchallenged in situations where social inequalities are easily
justified and calls for racial justice are seen as distasteful and unnecessary.[26] Built on a system of inequitable distribution, these forms of
racism protect a racist educational system by minimizing the effects of
racialized social systems in which economic, educational, political, and
social ideologies routinely advantage White people, while producing
adverse outcomes for URM groups.[27]

Structural racism has far-reaching consequences that affect housing,
health care, education, employment, earnings, benefits, credit, media,
politics, criminal justice, and premature death.[28] In educational settings, structural racism often goes unnoticed. People accept the practices that breed *institutional racism* (e.g., discriminatory policies and
inequitable opportunities for URMs perpetrated by schools, corporations, and other institutions) without considering how they give certain
groups the upper hand and oppress, marginalize, and silence others.[29]
Institutional actors use the institution's power to maintain the status
quo based on race and other social identities. In many STEM environments, values like competition, survival of the fittest, meritocracy,

individualism, and working to exhaustion are presented as normal Eurocentric characteristics of hard-working STEMers, which reinforces these STEM systems of White privilege and URM group marginalization.[30] Institutional racism also manifests in the perspectives, norms, and values that influence an institution's laws, policies, and systems of evaluation, often founded on Eurocentric principles. A disproportionate number of White male board members and endowed chairs is another expression of institutional racism. In contrast, when students of color talk about equity, they can be labeled radicals, subjected to surveillance, and sanctioned by university administrators and faculty.[31]

THE FINANCIAL FALLOUT FROM STRUCTURAL RACISM

Over the years, structural racism in this country has had a serious financial impact on people of color. A premier example is the long-standing discrepancy in state funding between some HBCUs and HWIs.[32] The Hatch Act of 1887 requires states to match federal education dollars at land-grant colleges, which were set up to teach agriculture, science, military science, and engineering. Tennessee has two land-grant colleges: the HBCU Tennessee State University (TSU) and the HWI University of Tennessee Knoxville. In 1934, the state legislature awarded UT Knoxville $450,000 but gave TSU just $52,000—a severe funding disparity that persists to this day. Between 2000 and 2016, TSU was shorted about $37 million because the state did not match federal funds.[33] In another example of widely disparate state subsidies, the HWIs University of North Carolina at Chapel Hill and North Carolina State University received about $15,700 per student in state funding in 2007, which is almost double the per-pupil subsidies awarded to two HBCUs, North Carolina A&T State University and Fayetteville State University.[34] Disparities like these contribute to the outsize debt that

URM students amass during their education, such as the 32 percent greater median debt that Black graduates of HBCUs carry compared to graduates of other nonprofit four-year schools.[35]

The situation is getting worse, due in part to legislation that has lapsed because of false claims that racism has ceased to exist and affirmative action policies are unfair and unnecessary. As of late 2019, minority-serving institutions and tribal colleges and universities (which educate more than four million students per year) were in jeopardy of losing $255 million as a result of their mandatory federal funding being allowed to expire.[36] Such structurally racist state funding and debt systems take a heavy toll on URM students and the institutions that serve them; if these funding inequities were righted, minority-serving institutions could increase the number of URMs who graduate with STEM PhDs.

Racially disparate compensation for STEM employment is another area showing the effects of structural racism. As of 2016, the median earnings of Blacks ($58,000) and Hispanics ($60,758) working in STEM occupations significantly lagged those of Whites ($71,897) and Asians ($90,000). On average, Black STEM workers earn 81 percent of their White counterparts' pay.[37] The disparity holds for science and engineering PhDs working full-time. According to a study by the National Science Board, in 2015 Black doctoral degree holders earned 35 percent less ($55,000); Latinxs, 28 percent less ($59,000); and Alaska Natives, 23 percent less ($62,000) than Whites with the same level of education ($78,000), while Asian Americans earned 9 percent more than Whites ($85,000).[38]

Graduate study requires time and money, so the financial picture for URMs in advanced STEM programs would be incomplete without examining education debt, which also shows marked discrepancies along racial and ethnic lines. Generally, STEM PhDs of color graduate with more debt than do White and Asian PhDs. Within the past ten years, 49 percent of Black STEM doctoral degree recipients accrued educational debt, as opposed to the 27 percent of non-URM recipients with any outstanding student loans. In the same groups, URMs were more than twice as likely as non-URMs (25 percent versus 10 percent) to report student loan debt over $30,000.[39]

EUGENICS:
THE PSEUDOSCIENCE THAT REFUSES TO DIE

Countless fields in higher education are founded on and continue to rely on White male supremacy, which reflects beliefs about the genetic inferiority of non-White people and promotes White domination.[40] The "science" of eugenics is a movement born in the aftermath of the Civil War that divided racial characteristics into "desirable" and "undesirable" categories so as to advance qualities associated with White people.[41]

Scientific racism, otherwise known as eugenics, flourished in the late nineteenth and early twentieth centuries and was designed to reflect socially constructed ideas of Black genetic inferiority that socially, materially, and scientifically advanced White hegemony.[42] Eugenics, which attempted to legitimize using selective breeding to improve the health and fitness of humankind, emphasized the superiority of White and middle- or upper-class genes and the social menace of inferior genes—that is, those of Black people of any class. The few "Black exhibits" who displayed "singular genius" were considered exceptions within their race, but Blacks were generally deemed inferior to Whites despite demonstrated intellectual abilities.[43]

A century ago, American colleges and universities acted on eugenic principles when they barred non-White groups from admission—and thereby from acquiring the knowledge and experience necessary to refute such beliefs. The eugenic tradition continues to shape postsecondary education and beyond even after the belief system was discredited.[44] More than a century after eugenics was introduced in the United States, the typical STEM college student remains White, male, and middle class, along with some students of Asian descent (e.g., Chinese and Indian).[45] One group of educational researchers described the STEM arena as an example of White institutional spaces that dovetail with eugenic principles:

> Such spaces are characterized by (1) the exclusion of those who are not White from positions of power, (2) the development of a White frame that organizes the logic of these institutions and normalizes White racial superiority, (3) the historical construction of a curricular model based on the thinking of White elites, and (4) the assertion of knowledge and knowledge production as neutral and unconnected to power relations.[46]

This is a sweet arrangement if you believe that White people are genetically superior to all other races and ethnic groups, but structural racism is what it really is. Structural racism in STEM often manifests as meritocracy and color blindness.[47] Although STEM is marketed as a competitive field that rewards only the deserving, research has shown even greater bias in STEM professions than in their non-STEM counterparts.[48] STEM education takes place in a culture that downplays both structural racism and students' raced and gendered identities, which implies that students' success relies only on their individual intelligence.[49] It is a convenient approach for universities because it shifts responsibility for recruiting and retaining URM STEM students into a mythical pipeline and allows administrators to ignore the racialized bias at work in their STEM departments and programs, which leads to the labeling of URM students as deficient and blaming them for their lack of representation.[50]

When students of color are made to feel responsible for their own underrepresentation in STEM fields, whether they attribute their academic troubles to their own deficiencies or to external structural barriers, both results can lead to depression, elevated stress levels, and other psychological problems, as well as poor academic performance.[51] Therapists grounded in cultural and racial educational expertise might be able to help URM students identify less obvious evidence of racism in their environments and to depersonalize these invalidating experiences while reinforcing their self-efficacy and STEM identities.[52] Such psychosocial support is critical for URM students because strengthening their science identities makes it more likely the students will persist in their academic programs.[53] Mentors of URM students and minoritized faculty members could also learn this type of intervention to extend its benefits more broadly.

LOOKING TOWARD HBCUS FOR GUIDANCE IN REVERSING STRUCTURAL RACISM IN STEM

Instead of assuming that HWIs will lead efforts to diversify STEM higher education, researchers could be studying the leadership styles and strategies of HBCUs. Although they are a tiny proportion of US educational institutions, HBCUs account for 17 percent of all bachelor's degrees earned by Blacks and 24 percent of all degrees earned by Blacks in STEM fields.[54] These highly effective institutions succeed in spite of limited budgets and endowments, and they take Black students that many HWIs would reject. Black HBCU graduates are more likely to be thriving and financially solvent than Black graduates who did not receive their degrees from HBCUs.[55] It stands to reason, then, that we can learn from HBCUs' successes to produce a new generation of STEMers of color.

FACULTY OVERWHELMED BY SERVICE WORK, VOLUNTARY AND IMPOSED

Retaining Black and other URM faculty is clearly critical to recruiting and retaining URM students in STEM disciplines. As my colleagues and I have outlined, one Black professor can teach hundreds of students in the course of a career, and some of those students will become professors, who will teach hundreds more students and encourage even more future professionals in their disciplines.[56] Through the service of a single professor, great intellectual and technological change can arise. A major drain on these faculty members' time, however, is uncompensated, race-related, service expectations, also called invisible labor, such as leading campus and administrative diversity efforts and serving on diversity-related departmental and university committees and task forces. Lessening the strain of this service would allow more faculty-initiated service based on their own missions and expertise to improve equity in educational spaces and more time for professorial work. This change would help to stop the revolving door in which URM faculty leave the professoriat not long after entering it.

As Amado Padilla observed, Black faculty may be involved in service commitments more "to ensure the perceived fairness of the process (e.g., hiring search committee) than the end result (i.e., who is hired)."[57] In this way, institutions tend to overuse their tokenized faculty of color to create the illusion of diversity without actually incorporating these faculty members' goals and perspectives.[58] After all, their service is invaluable to their institutions. As one researcher remarked, "The hands-on attention that many [minoritized] professors willingly provide [to students of color] is an unheralded linchpin in institutional efforts to create an inclusive learning environment and to keep students enrolled."[59]

Three colleagues and I investigated service related to increasing Black participation in their discipline by Black engineering and computing PhD students, postdocs, pretenure and tenured faculty, minority engineering program directors, and engineering or university administrators.[60] These activities demand an extra expenditure of time and energy, which is often not considered in decisions on tenure or promotion.[61] In our study, participants distinguished between "voluntold" service (initiated by their employer) and their self-initiated or voluntary service. Eighteen of the thirty-seven participants (49 percent) described feeling external pressure to take part in university or departmental service associated with efforts to recruit underrepresented students. One of them, Dr. Heed, said:

> One of the things that is important is that if you're an underrepresented faculty member, and that could be female or African American or American Indian or whatever, the administration tends to look to you to help with a lot of activities that they don't ask the White US males to do. Because they're interested in diversity and they ask you to do all things in diversity, and they want you if they have an event or whatever.

If Dr. Heed skipped one of his university's innumerable meetings concerning several diversity initiatives, his colleagues would later ask where he had been. He was often anxious about these obligations, which he described as opportunities for the department to appear diverse, and he was well aware of his hypervisibility as the only tenured Black faculty member of his engineering and computing department. Dr. Boyd, a pretenure professor, had similar experiences, which interfered with his research and did little to advance his career:

> Just because your department head feels good about you when you do something [diversity related] doesn't mean it's going to help you to get tenure. Because it's not just the department head that votes for your tenure; it's the other tenured faculty members. And if you're

not doing things to impress them, you will not get the vote that you really need to get tenure.

Our team of researchers concluded that going along with voluntold service requests to speak for people of color further tokenizes faculty members and can make them feel exploited. It also adds to the service they don't have to be asked to do because they feel strongly motivated to provide it: advising and guiding students of color. The time constraints resulting from voluntold and voluntary service made some of our participants feel highly ambivalent about mentoring.

Students of color often seek out mentors of color, which means that a URM faculty member can become overwhelmed by a large number of mentees. Colleagues might advise them to limit the number of mentees they take on, but, as one associate professor of plant biology put it, "It's very, very difficult if you're an African American, and an African American student comes to you, and you know that there are no other avenues for them, another person [Black faculty] that they could find. So, I actually have a hard time saying no to students."

For example, Dr. Dezman was mentoring twice the number of students that his colleagues were. He said:

> Since I'm the only African American faculty member and you have ten African American students, then they all want to do research with you. They all want letters. They all want you to facilitate them. And there is nothing wrong with that. But I would just need a more equitable workload . . . So, I feel burden[ed] from that point of view. It's like I have to . . . overcompensate here.

As soon as they are hired, faculty of color often feel pressured to help fix their institution's lack of diversity. Generally, the diversity-increasing strategies are designed with little or no input from members of the targeted groups, so the new faculty may feel additionally burdened with carrying out activities they suspect will not work. Such requests for service come from the highest offices and are therefore not easy to turn down. All of it—the virtually mandated service to the institution and the heart-driven service to students of color—detracts from URM faculty's research, scholarship, and even their teaching and puts them at a disadvantage to their less-burdened non-URM colleagues. Is it therefore any wonder that the number of US faculty of color, especially in STEM fields, remains so low?

CHAPTER THREE

The Stress of Success for the Underrepresented and Minoritized in STEM

AT A NATIONAL CONFERENCE on engineering education, I had just wrapped up my presentation of research on racist and sexist experiences of Black women doctoral students in engineering when a White man from the audience approached me. Speaking of his fellow engineering professors, he said:

> Look, I'm going to tell you what they won't say. We are competitive with *each other*. We will cut *each other's* throat in a heartbeat if it benefits our research. We don't care about failing half of our students, and they are most likely White or foreigners, so why would we care about failing Black students? Honestly, we just call them quota kids anyway. Besides, we already got diversity 'cause we got a few women [engineering faculty]. But they are both bitches [*laughing*].

The White engineering professor's appraisal of his department reveals a brutal environment where "diversity" means having two (despised and ridiculed) women professors. Faculty compete fiercely for recognition and grant money, guard turf, and cultivate hard personas. Hypermasculine posturing and power seeking are actually part of the DNA of engineering culture.[1] As the man said, in this toxic atmosphere designed to weed students out, one can hardly expect instructors to empathize with Black students, who are stereotyped as "quota kids": those whose places in the engineering program are supposedly unearned. The baseline is a foundational structure that was never meant to include URM students and women and that has plagued STEM departments since their creation.

The experiences of my study participants show how students experience education in engineering and other STEM disciplines. Rasheeda was a third-year Black student in computer information systems engineering at an HBCU, which, as is typical of current STEM departments at HBCUs, had largely international White and Asian faculty. She explained that her early life had prepared her for an engineering program:

> It's like the only reason I'm able to survive this chaos is because of the background that I have. I'm used to being in an environment where it ain't no love here, it ain't no support. I come from the streets. There's no love out there. There is no support. There's no friends. People will tell you one thing and do something different. They will smile at you and smack you in the back of the head with a brick when you turn your back. All of those elements are here, except here all the actors are White [or] Asian, and mostly male.

I have heard many URM and Asian students in a broad sample of STEM disciplines report their struggles in a climate characterized by racialized assaults and stereotypes. Asians, for example, are often preoccupied with striving to uphold the stereotype that they are inherently great at STEM subjects. Some students manage to develop more sophisticated coping strategies and professional identities, although their daily academic lives remain stressful. Despite getting excellent grades, coveted STEM internships, and recognized scholarship, URM students can never avoid being seen as intellectually less than their White and Asian peers or positioned as anomalous. This chapter focuses primarily on experiences reported by URM students in engineering and mathematics disciplines.

HOW STEREOTYPING WORKS

The students I interviewed did not need prompts from me to suggest that their computing and engineering classrooms were awash in stereotypes.[2] Most students said racial stereotypes were omnipresent. In one study, my coauthor and I found that stereotyping or the threat of being stereotyped was ubiquitous, particularly at HWIs.[3] Isolation intensified this experience because students felt more stereotyped when only a few or no other people of their racial group were present. Even when they received the highest grades in the class, they felt they had to continually prove their intellectual abilities, which meant studying unrelentingly and having little time to enjoy their subject matter or their academic achievements. This occurs because once the stereotype has been triggered and perceived as a racialized threat, it stays active long after the event in which the student was stereotyped.

In research settings, stereotypes and other forms of racialized bias have been activated simply by having students identify their race on a test. A single glance or word can set off the stereotype in a person who holds that stereotype. For those who are the subject of stereotyping, it is there every time they appear in public; it colors their every movement. Stereotypes can be activated even in the absence of any immediate stimulus. A URM grad student doing homework in her apartment, for example, is still plagued by the expectation that her colleagues will assume that her work is subpar; if it's exemplary, however, her instructor or fellow students will question where she "found" the correct answers. Although she is in her home, away from those who disbelieve her abilities, she cannot escape stereotyping linked to her race and gender because her environment constantly reinforces it.

Stereotypes have the most sway among members of the socially dominant group, who readily see members of their own group as individuals with unique traits but believe absurdities such as most Asians

are inherently good at mathematics and most Blacks are innately incapable of it.[4] Racial stereotypes often presume negative attributes such
as intellectual inferiority, criminal behavior, and laziness for an entire
subject group, with anomalies being cast as exceptional. Without training to challenge what one "knows" to be true, stereotypes can remain
permanent structures in the human mind.

THE POWER OF STEREOTYPES:
WHATEVER DOESN'T KILL YOU GIVES YOU
UNHEALTHY COPING MECHANISMS

STEM higher education is full of race-related discriminatory barriers
that can damage the health and well-being of students of color, and
racial stereotyping is at the heart of this discrimination. Racial stereotyping systematically marginalizes URM students by endorsing negative expectations in educational settings.[5] Through the medium of
racial microaggressions (e.g., looks of disbelief when URM students
walk into an advanced math class, false accusations of cheating, and
repeatedly having their comments ignored in small-group work), stereotypes exclude URM STEM students and cause racial anxiety, minority status stress, and a desire to abandon the STEM arena.[6]

The stress of living in a racist society and having that racism directed
against oneself is quantifiable: high blood pressure and temporary loss
of working memory are two documented physical effects.[7] The condition is called allostasis, a state of constant physiological alarm caused
by elevated levels of adrenaline, the stress hormone produced when we
sense danger.[8] To step away from STEM environments for a moment,
one consequence of racism in the United States is the high rates of African American newborn and maternal death (twice those of the White
population), which remain high even when all other factors are controlled. African women who give birth in the United States, however,

have the same newborn and maternal death rates as Whites do—until they have been here for a while. After twenty years in the United States, the Africans' maternal and infant death rates are the same as those of African Americans.[9] In other words, people from countries with homogeneous populations of color (in which interpersonal racism plays a much smaller role than it does in the United States) do not experience the stress of discrimination by race until they have spent enough time here to get the full experience of American racism.

A recent study of forty-eight Black engineering and computing doctoral students deepened my understanding of the dynamics at work in this population.[10] Although my colleagues and I had not approached this study expecting to make race the primary issue, the students described their experiences mainly through the perspective of race. For them, racialized experiences often caused stress, strain, academic performance anxiety, and doubts about their qualifications. The racial composition of students' academic environments and the racialized culture of engineering and computing departments seemed to intensify impostor syndrome (i.e., feeling that one is perceived as a fraud in spite of high achievement in one's academic specialty). The coping mechanisms these students used also took a toll on them.

Several themes emerged with haunting regularity from interviews with these students, who were studying in eleven geographically disparate institutions. The chief patterns we found were self-blame and self-questioning (impostor syndrome), overworking in the hope of having their competence recognized, going into survival mode, experiencing racial battle fatigue, and being underemployed as a direct result of being denied opportunities by White or Asian principal investigators. URM women doctoral students reported experiences that reflected the double bind of racism and sexism. The strain of operating in primarily White- and male-dominated departments made these URM students question their right to be where they were.

Overwork and Racial Battle Fatigue

STEM doctoral programs are challenging for everyone, but 81 percent of our participants saw themselves as working "twice as hard" as their Asian and White fellow students in order to prove their worth to professors and peers, who they felt doubted their abilities. They maintained a constant presence in the lab, sacrificing weekends and holidays, in hopes that their extra labor would demonstrate a strong work ethic and engender a sense of belonging. No matter what they do, however, many URM students never feel that they fully belong where they have every right to be.

Another response to the trauma of surviving in a racialized climate is racial battle fatigue (discussed in chapter 2). Racial battle fatigue in an educational setting can make people feel powerless, invisible, or forced to represent one's group.[11] Symptoms of anger, escapism, withdrawal, and frustration mounted as our study participants gave up on thriving in their programs and concentrated on simply surviving. Racial battle fatigue causes some Black students to work unrelentingly, which results in psychological, emotional, and physical trauma, stress, and strain. It can result from microaggressions, including backhanded compliments like "You're smart for a Black girl."

For some study participants who were also war veterans, their STEM experience was disturbingly familiar. Derek, a sixth-year aerospace engineering PhD student, said that doctoral training in aerospace engineering reminded him of the military, where soldiers were expected to work to exhaustion:

> In hindsight this [combat in Iraq] is what it [doctoral training] looks like . . . You're being told, "What graduate students do is they sleep in the lab." You need to be tired and disheveled and if you're not, you're not passionate about the work. You don't put in enough time. And you're like, "Well, okay" . . . But then it does do something to

your psyche and to your . . . I mean, it could make you stronger, but it does damage you in some way, internally like, you know, "How am I going to deal with this?"

John Henryism and Resilience

Overworking is also visible in the behavior pattern called "John Henryism." Public health researcher Dr. Sherman James originated the term when he was studying African Americans' coping strategies after prolonged exposure to social stresses due to racism and discrimination.[12] He named the condition for the folklore character John Henry, an African American laborer who tried to beat the pace of a mechanical steel-driver with nothing but a hammer and his own strong body. John Henry won the contest, only to collapse and die from the superhuman effort he had made. High-achieving Blacks often adopt John Henryism as a coping strategy, pursuing goals so strenuously that they sometimes sacrifice personal relationships and health.[13] Race-related stress and anxiety in this group have been associated with a high level of stress-related illnesses.[14]

Working to exhaustion can start in childhood, as Gene Brody and colleagues found in some African American youths they followed for five years.[15] Although these students were identified as resilient, they experienced tremendous internal pressure to succeed, such as being the first in their family to graduate from college or land a white-collar job. Internal pressures, coupled with the flagrant daily racism and discrimination they withstood, often caused them to neglect sleep, exercise, and other self-care, which led to disproportionately high rates of health problems, including obesity and high blood pressure. Also, levels of the stress hormones cortisol, adrenaline, and noradrenaline were higher in the resilient study participants than in those not identified as resilient. This finding suggests that the quality of resilience or grit, which is supposed to ensure academic success for URM students in STEM, is hardly the panacea it has been claimed to be.[16] Instead, it seems more like an unhealthy indicator of the pressure to succeed felt by Black and other URM students. Asking URM students to continually be resilient and rise above racist polices, practices, and actions over and over again without appropriate supports is in actuality a form of oppression, with outcomes that can be deleterious and at worst deadly.

Self-Doubt, Self-Blame, and Impostor Syndrome

The students in our study censured themselves or questioned their abilities in the racialized culture of their departments. The absence of Black or URM faculty and peers worsened their persistent feelings of inadequacy and questioning of their abilities. Impostor syndrome is the feeling of being perceived as fraudulent or undeserving of one's place despite high achievement in one's academic domain.[17] URMs who fail to internalize their documented academic success question their own abilities and view themselves as impostors. An alternate and more likely reading is that URMs *are* positioned as impostors.

My personal experience is relevant here. The students' reports of feeling unqualified and undeserving of their departmental positions took me back to a job I held at Agilent Technologies, a subsidiary of Hewlett-Packard. My White male manager, in an email copied needlessly to a couple of other White males, asked a cryptic technical question that was purposely confusing and awkwardly worded. When I responded by asking him to clarify, he didn't. At that point, I was sure I had been set up. From that day on, he treated me as if I did not know engineering. I was laid off a few weeks later.

Survival Mode

Our study participants spoke of "pushing through" (i.e., ignoring as best they could) distressing negative encounters, including racialized experiences. This also meant ignoring their health, including activities that kept them healthy (e.g., working out, volunteering, attending to their spiritual lives). Some students went into survival mode, which they had developed from coping with earlier trauma. Racially insensitive STEM incidents in their undergraduate education had prepared them for doctoral survival mode (prevalent mostly at HWIs, but also present at some HBCUs).

Almost half of our participants spoke of persevering through similar racially hostile academic environments and situations, some through their entire academic careers. Their personal history of always rising above let them call on the resilience they had developed in order to survive, but the accompanying stress tempered their success. Resilience is an admirable quality, but it cannot be used as a rationale to dismiss the seriousness of long-term mental health problems and critical race-conscious support systems to assist in ensuring students' healthy participation in STEM.

The Double Bind of URM Women STEM Students

In 1976, Shirley Malcom, Paula Hall, and Janet Brown, while exploring the status of minority women in science, introduced the term *double bind*.[18] Our study participants who were also mothers were subject to what we call a triple bind, as motherhood added another layer of bias to their already racist gendered encounters. Rasheeda, a mother as well as a graduate student in computer information systems engineering, felt that her Blackness, her gender, and motherhood added burdens that Black women doctoral students without children did not endure. Her preoccupation with research and study tasks eventually compromised her parenting: "What that really boils down to is it stretches outside of this environment. I'm sitting on the couch, racking my brain on how to finish something, and my children are trying to interact, and I have nothing to give them because I'm pouring everything into this."[19] Rasheeda was married, but single URM STEM student mothers experience yet another layer of bias based on societal judgments of their unwed mother status, for an intersectional dividend.

In another study, my coauthor and I found that the effect of meritocratic and color-blind spaces can result in women of color feeling as though their frustrations are unacknowledged. One student recalled that her adviser, a White man, told her to forget about her gender and the color of her skin and just focus on the subject.[20] By doing this, he ignored the intersectionality of her gendered and raced experience within her PhD program and negated the importance of her identity. In a study on the effects of race and gender in engineering education, we labeled the experiences of Black women in engineering PhD programs or postdoctoral positions as the "female engineering experience," highlighting structural issues such as hostile, unsupportive environments; a complete absence or very low numbers of Black women in engineering faculty roles; gendered stereotypes ingrained and accepted within the engineering program; and exclusion (e.g., by the "male huddle," in which men collaborate only with each other).[21]

Much of the literature on stereotype management assumes that coping strategies such as overwork, survival mode, and John Henryism are consciously adopted. The presumption is that students who feel the weight of a stereotype choose to act in response to a stimulus that is creating psychological strain and then to select a coping strategy based on clear recognition and labeling of the stereotype. Our graduate student participants, however, felt generally stressed and anxious but could not always tell what had triggered those feelings. Developing and deploying strategies to manage the stressors was therefore not simple or straightforward, like trying to meditate or yoga your way out of feelings of impostorism.

Under the strain of existing in a racialized atmosphere, with constantly elevated adrenaline levels and pressure, URM students experience racial tension in their bodies. The discordance between the racial makeup of their academic environments and their racialized STEM identities appeared to exacerbate impostor phenomenon and performance anxiety.[22] Study participants were often unable to identify the racialized structural barriers embodied in cultural norms and institutional practices, which reflect both calculated and unintentional choices of institutional leaders and the interaction of cultural and institutional racism.[23] Without knowing the true sources of their anxiety, URM students in STEM disciplines do not usually choose a specific coping strategy from their library of strategies: generally they act more or less blindly and hope the stress will stop.

MANAGING STEREOTYPES

Some URM students do consciously use techniques for deflecting stereotypes, at least until they become so routine that they are performed automatically. Many of my research participants over the years have resorted to what they called *code-switching*, or alternating their customary way of speaking with the language of the dominant culture. A related term that many interviewees used is *frontin'*, or performing an act that the prevailing White culture can accept but that entails some sacrifice of personal identity. Every single participant in one of my studies mentioned examples of frontin' they had used to prevent or minimize race-based incidents they could reliably anticipate.[24] Most of them used frontin' tactics to combat racialized beliefs endemic to their majority-White school environments, but they emphasized that these strategies were not a natural part of their identity or behavior.

One type of frontin' was not wearing clothes associated with being a threat. As one URM student said, "One day I wore this nice red and blue Nike jumpsuit and a couple of White dudes said, 'You are confusing me. Are you Bloods or Crips?'" This "joking" remark lumps a

URM student in with street gangs who represent their gang status by their colors, but the subtext is that all students must conform to White self-presentation. When URM students can't even get dressed without anticipating a negative reaction, it is obvious that racial and ethnic stereotypes are always at work in their minds, siphoning energy away from their studies.

An opposite, more defiant frontin' technique also centered on clothing. In an attempt to hang on to their personal identity and resist demands for cultural assimilation, some students performed stereotypical notions of Blackness. Mike was one of three male students in the study who responded to racism by adopting a stereotypical Black appearance (e.g., wearing saggy jeans and Timberland boots or growing out their hair in an Afro). Mike dressed like this when he started college as a way of announcing his racial identity: "All these things I would say were attributed to African Americans I would do in school 'cause I felt like I needed to. And if I didn't do it, I felt like I was separating myself out, like I wasn't being true." With time and reflection, Mike began to distance himself from the obligation of performing the stereotypes for his own purposes. As a senior in college, he celebrated his Blackness by embracing a more personally authentic style.

Another way of frontin' that several students mentioned is smiling a lot and nodding in agreement in an effort to seem approachable. "I'm large, Black [referring to both his dark skin and his racial identity], and male, and I intimidate most Whites, and for that matter some Black people," said one student. "So my mom told me that I would have to walk through life with a big goofy smile on my face or the world would be scared of me." Large, young White men are not usually seen as threatening, but this Black man had to train himself to present a genial persona simply to move through daily life. Women of all races understand this, as most of us have heard variations on the male command to smile, often from total strangers. The common phrase "resting bitch face" suggests that an unsmiling female face is perceived as a threat to men. Whether someone tells them to smile or they decide to do it to make themselves less threatening or more appealing to the dominant group, URM members realize that how their presence is received is conditional on their facial expression.

Similar to constant smiling is excessive nodding to show understanding, even when they don't understand. One Black student spoke of a math class in which "sometimes it seems like they are watching me to make sure I get it or that I belong. It's like they are waiting for me to [#$%] up So I just nod no matter what . . . Then at an inconspicuous hour I go find the teaching assistant." It is unfairly burdensome—to say the least—to feel obliged to do one's real learning in private, after class, away from the judgment of others. STEM classrooms are rarely safe spaces for any students, but especially URM students, to ask questions that reveal less than perfect understanding and to get the teaching help they need to proceed to the next stage of learning. Thus, the need for learning spaces that allow vulnerability and forbid criticism or ridicule is critical to a healthy STEM education.

The majority of the Black students in most of my studies said that their concern with racial stereotypes had made them fixate on proving their value and defining themselves to an educational system that devalued them. However, even those who had tried hardest to assimilate spoke of the value and comfort they felt in being Black, which Latinx STEM students echoed. My Latinx participants also avoided revealing much about their personal lives in an attempt to mask huge race- and class-based gaps, such as hiding the fact that they worked all summer while classmates relaxed in their families' second homes.

One Latinx student learned the hard way to keep his personal life private. Jose was a second-year physics major doing research in a chemical engineering lab at a Hispanic-serving institution, one of thirty-eight high-achieving Black or Latinx undergraduates whom I interviewed for a study.[25] Everyone else in his lab was Asian or White. In this lab, students took turns choosing music to play, and when Jose's turn arrived, he was eager to share a favorite salsa CD. For the first thirty seconds of music, total silence reigned, and then the lab burst out laughing, as though someone had told a joke. They imitated salsa dancing, called each other *ese* ("Hey bro"), and acted out a gang gun battle. Jose grabbed his CD and fled. The next three weeks of constant teasing caused him to leave that lab, even though he had liked the research he had done there. His reaction to the experience was especially severe because he had finally felt as if the original lab accepted him. The lab he transferred to made Jose feel welcome, but his new principal investigator cautioned him not to be "too sensitive about jokes and good-natured fun."

Before this incident, Jose had felt sheltered from stereotypes, but now his guard was up. He dodged any mention of Latinx culture and didn't play his music anywhere near his engineering classmates. To short-circuit stereotypes about young unmarried Latinas bearing children, Jose hid his girlfriend's pregnancy. Jose was one of twelve study participants who were considering abandoning a STEM career path altogether to escape being stereotyped and racially assaulted. The majority of the twelve feared that racialized stereotyping would haunt them no matter how many STEM degrees or accolades they received.

BUILDING STRONG STEM IDENTITIES: TWO CASE STUDIES

STEM identities are fluid, continuous, dynamic, and often situational. As a mathematics identity develops, for example, one becomes more assured in one's identity as a doer, or owner-operator, of mathematics. Forming a solid STEM identity has been shown to be a critical factor for URM students' success in STEM.[26] However, students of color often have trouble forming a healthy, functional STEM identities because they encounter stereotyped beliefs about their abilities and feel powerless to counter those attitudes. In the worst case, they conclude that the stereotype is accurate and they really are constitutionally incapable of doing STEM.

The research trend is to explore the failure of students of color in STEM while ignoring those who have excelled in math-dependent disciplines, but my work opposes that trend. Instead, I focus on the trials and rewards of URM students who excel in all measures of traditional definitions of academic success (e.g., high STEM GPAs, internships, high standardized test scores), who earn their degrees and move into professions or professorships. Here I analyze the academic biographies of two high-achieving Black STEM professionals, Tinesha and Rob. I came to know them through a study of how Black mathematics students develop robust mathematical identities in a racialized college environment.[27] As I noticed patterns of coping and resilience in the retrospective accounts of twenty-three high-achieving Black STEM students' educational careers, similar pictures of their vulnerability, challenges, and supports emerged. The students themselves identified these risk and protective factors. In the course of analyzing the factors they identified, I isolated three major features of weaker and stronger mathematical identities (see table 3.1).

After analyzing the study results, I chose to profile two study participants whose experiences encapsulated those of most participants. At the time of our interviews, Tinesha had earned a master's degree in bioengineering and completed her first year as a graduate student in mathematics education at a Midwestern university. Rob had a PhD in applied mathematics in addition to three master's degrees and was an assistant professor at an HBCU. Each of them had started with comparatively weak strategies for dealing with racialized attitudes at school.

TABLE 3.1

Major features of fragile and robust mathematics identities

Fragile mathematics identity	Robust mathematics identity
Defends oneself against racialized attitudes by demonstrating mathematical achievement	Defines oneself by enjoying and embracing mathematics
Responds in the moment to racialized experiences (reactive)	Uses stable, clever, coping strategies to defend against racialized mathematical experiences
High achieving in mathematics but externally focused and bittersweet	Internally focused and affirming of their own and others' successful mathematical outcomes

Source: E. O. McGee, "Robust and Fragile Mathematics Identities: A Framework for Exploring Racialized Experiences and High Achievement among Black College Students," *Journal of Research in Mathematics Education 46*, no. 5 (2015): 599–625, http://www.nctm.org/Publications/Journal-for-Research-in-Mathematics-Education/2015/Vol46/Issue5/Robust-and-Fragile-Mathematical-Identities_-A-Framework-for-Exploring-Racialized-Experiences-and-High-Achievement-Among-Black-College-Students/.

"Why Are All the White Kids Smart and All the Black Kids Dumb?"

Both Tinesha and Rob spoke of being the targets of academic bias at various times in their lives. For part of his childhood, Rob lived in a highly diverse neighborhood, which, in his words, was "cleverly disguised to perpetuate shrewd racial and even shrewder class divisions." By the third grade, he saw a pattern in his integrated school, and one day he asked his mother, "Why are all the White kids smart and all the Black kids dumb?" In response to the problem, he made it his mission to prove the stereotype about Black kids wrong. Mathematics seemed to be the subject most likely to make his talents shine, so that is where he concentrated his efforts, with his mother's encouragement.

In his sixth-grade math class, the teacher tracked students by seating them at one of five tables that reflected their ability. She placed him at the second-highest mathematics table. Rob argued that his consistently high math grades had earned him a seat at the highest table, which was all White and Asian students, but the teacher refused to move him. When he continued to object, she sent him to the principal's office. Once, when he got angry enough to walk out of the classroom, flinging his arms and stomping his feet, he was banned from class for several days. Later, Rob felt he had missed out on having almost perfect scores because of that experience, but he was proud that he had stood up to the racist actions of this White teacher. As in other early school experiences, his reaction protected his mathematical identity but ultimately set him back academically or did him psychological harm.

In her mostly Black neighborhood, Tinesha had been a high achiever whose teachers acknowledged her intelligence. She held leadership positions in high school and got good summer jobs, but her success and self-esteem were unstable. She secretly worried that her teachers' admiration would disappear with one bad grade. This fear only intensified in college, where she felt obligated to prove she belonged on campus and in these classrooms. She also felt a new pressure for the first time:

> I came to realize these people [college administrators, teachers, and her peers] don't expect too much of me in this class . . . I've always had this idea, even when I was younger, like in elementary school, if you tell me that I can't do something, then I want to prove to you that I can.

In her advanced calculus course, for example, Tinesha answered several introductory questions correctly. With a look of astonishment, the teacher said, "Wow, that's right. And Tinesha, no one helped you with the answer?" She held back her tears until class was over, but anger and embarrassment kept her away from the class for a week. Her self-defeating method of coping with insulting treatment exemplifies a fragile mathematics identity.

Tinesha's firm intention to master mathematics in order to prove the stereotype wrong had carried her through high school. Rob had focused on math to demonstrate to others his competencies and satisfy his mother, who saw mathematical achievement as proof of his intellectual ability and a ticket to a good career. External motivations like these, however, would not be enough for the long haul. To persist through college and beyond, Rob and Tinesha had to find inner motivation and come to embrace math, finding joy and satisfaction in the discipline. This protected them from future challenges, such as having to prove themselves to every new round of teachers, peers, administrators, and internship supervisors.

Racially biased events in a student's life can be unpredictable and lead to anger, frustration, and despair. Rob and Tinesha suggested that racist acts would always hurt, no matter how good they got at coping with them. At different points in their undergraduate years, both students decided that trying to rid the entire educational system of stereotypes and other forms of bias was not the best use of their time and energy. When Rob won a college scholarship to a university known for producing world-class mathematicians, at first he accepted the messages he got that affirmative action had been the main reason for his admission. Then he recognized that internalizing this stereotype was eroding his mathematical and racial identities. His solution was to leave that university for a less prestigious STEM-intensive institution in a racially diverse city, where both his mathematics and racial identities thrived.

As the only Black student in many of her engineering courses, Tinesha detected an exclusionary attitude from professors and other students: "And if you ask me for instances, I can give you a couple, but [mostly] it's the looks they give me. I know I'm not crazy. And [I] see them looking at me and they are saying, 'You don't really belong here.'"

Building a Protective Identity to Promote an Internalized Alliance with STEM Success

For Rob and Tinesha, their successes were not as fulfilling as they had imagined because they constantly anticipated the next experience of being devalued. Drawing on their passion for mathematics and engineering as a motivation, however, served to strengthen their mathematical identities. As their math identities became more robust, Rob and Tinesha learned how to handle racially charged situations in a mathematics setting in ways that did not jeopardize their academic success. With time, they both developed a deep appreciation of math, doing math "just for the fun of it" (Rob) and seeking out peers and organizations that nourished their mathematical and racial identities. This process involved self-discovery and self-definition based on associating with like-minded mentors, students, and community and college organizations. Tinesha took classes in African studies that helped her to heal the racial wounds. Both Tinesha and Rob joined organizations that celebrated Black STEM students' identities or honored STEM achievement.[28]

As they worked on themselves, their methods of dealing with stigma and bias became more sophisticated. For example, Rob often wore T-shirts with sayings like "Danger: Educated Black Man." He embraced racialized comedy (e.g., Dave Chappelle, Chris Rock, the satirical publication the *Onion*), which relieved his stress and gave him solace through shared experiences of marginalization. With determination and resourcefulness, Rob and Tinesha worked to build a durable, robust mathematical identity that helped to shield them from racial stereotypes.

At one time, they had responded to stereotypes and bias by with-drawing in silent anger or becoming depressed, but now they had become adept at using humor and clever strategies. They could deliver pointed retorts and then return matter-of-factly to the task at hand. Learning how to manipulate stereotypes helped Tinesha handle racial-ized encounters in research positions:

> I love my research and I know I deserve to be doing this work. Some-times the others in the lab will ask me one of those "What is it like to be Black" questions, like "How did it feel to live around gang-bangers?" Then I ask them, "Well, how did it feel to be privileged and not really struggle for anything?" That shuts them down fairly quickly. But I always continue to talk with them as if we did not just insult each other and that actually helps to smooth things over for the most part. But there are always a couple [colleagues] that wouldn't give me the time of day.

Tinesha's strategy of trading stereotypes made it clear that both par-ties' experiences can be misrepresented and helped to clear the air so work could proceed. And although she knew some colleagues disdained her, she didn't make it her business to change them, which saved her some aggravation.

In graduate school, Rob continued to field belittling "jokes" and discriminatory attitudes. When his applied mathematics professor asked him if he knew any "good cleaning ladies or maybe one of your relatives might be in a need of a job," Rob replied that all his fam-ily members had master's degrees. Though it hurt that his mathemat-ics professor would reduce the women in his family to stereotypical roles, he decided to tolerate it. As long as his intellectual ability was accepted, Rob could "put up with smart fools making racially stupid assumptions."

Thus, the robust mathematical identities Tinesha and Rob constructed allowed them to operate from a position of strength instead of being drained by constant striving to demonstrate their intelligence. Their extensive personal work also spared them the psychological cost of choked-back sadness or anger. Racialized experiences still happened, but their sophisticated ways of responding took a lighter toll on their equilibrium. The mixture of strategies they used minimized the psychological damage associated with being a high achiever in a field in which negative racial stereotypes exist and allowed them to maintain positive attitudes and behaviors.

As Rob's and Tinesha's coping mechanisms developed, mathematics changed from a way of demonstrating their intelligence to a tool for understanding, knowing, and serving others. Stronger mathematical or STEM identities and high-level coping skills allow vulnerable students to maintain emotional stability while minimizing, yet never fully eliminating, the emotional drain associated with in-the-moment responses. Their strengthened math identities also uncovered a drive to teach and mentor younger students in math and engineering and help them develop their passions. I call this form of mathematical identity "robust" because mathematical achievement that is internally motivated and supplemented by emotionally healthy networks is self-affirming and sustainable.

However, I want to caution readers that these two narratives of mathematics and engineering robustness, which include an evolution of strategies that ultimately lessened the blunt force of racism, must not be perceived as a way of "fixing" other URM students. It's a shame that these two brilliant people had to expend energy defending their place in STEM fields; Tinesha and Rob should not have the burden of tweaking their responses to racist encounters in order to minimize collateral damage. This is extra work that their brains could be using to do something else, such as helping us fly in our cars. The culture of STEM departments must be indicted and completely revamped to accept the full humanity of URM people in STEM. I have a plan for that (see chapter 6).

CHAPTER FOUR

Why Justice-Oriented STEM Is the Key to Getting and Keeping Students of Color in STEM and—Oh Yeah, Saving Our Planet Too!

You know, what separates me from another person is probably one thousandth of a certain segment of genes, and we're all relatively close together. If you look at history wisely . . . we descended from a bottleneck of around 2,000 [to] 3,000 individuals to the billions we have today. We're one big family and we're neglecting our cousins in a sense. I believe that's important, but saying this always gets me in trouble.

WITH THIS COMMENT, Miguel, a Latinx biology and physics major aiming for a PhD in physics, revealed a wish to use his science education to make positive contributions to society. Miguel's perspective is both informed and empathetic, but his broad view of our human responsibility to take care of one another is evidently controversial in his science department. His education has shown him that all people are closely connected genetically, but voicing those thoughts in the very environment in which he conceived them gets him "in trouble." Are compassion and wisdom such rare commodities in an institution of higher education, where one might expect those qualities to be desirable? Or could the trouble reside in his environment, where the individual takes center stage and competition is more the norm than cooperation?

Miguel is far from being alone. More than half the thirty-eight Black or Latinx college students my colleague and I interviewed from 2010 to 2012—college juniors and seniors with high GPAs—expressed a desire to use their STEM professional skills to give back to their own communities or to humanity in general. Most of the students of color I have interviewed for my research were not content merely to pursue high-paying, high-status professional STEM jobs: they also wanted to do good and be the good in the world. Using my own and others' research, I identified their common goal as a key motivator for URM students' perseverance in scientific and technical fields; I call it an equity ethic.[1]

An *equity ethic* is a set of moral values that includes a principled concern for justice, particularly racial justice, for addressing racial inequities, and for the well-being of people suffering under various inequities. STEM folks show their equity ethic as intentions or actions taken to use their STEM-specific skills and positions to address equity concerns. An equity ethic can manifest through research, teaching, mentoring, program administration, entrepreneurship, and leadership positions in justice-oriented organizations. It can also apply outside of work.

THE EQUITY ETHIC AS A MOTIVATOR
FOR MARGINALIZED STUDENTS

In a recent study, twenty-four of the thirty-eight URM students we interviewed spoke of wanting their work to help all people, but especially those with whom they share a culture or community.[2] Some participants broadly defined their communities as those that included other STEM students, humanity or society, the environment, others who have been marginalized, or their racial or ethnic group. Many spoke of mentoring and teaching in their STEM careers and disciplines in response to the lack of people in STEM who look like them. Their objectives blended collectivist and altruistic leanings, including a desire to help those who are not part of their immediate in-group; these students' sense of responsibility extended to all humanity but did not neglect those who have been racially marginalized. More than half of them planned to use their careers to tackle global health and quality-of-life issues. One such student was Vita, an African American physics major, who saw herself becoming an advocate for global health policy and exploring social, economic, environmental, and political variables that contribute to health disparities.

> The two things I'm really interested in are clinical trials . . . of implantable devices and things like that and targeted drug-delivery regimens . . . My passion for global health care policy is embedded [in the fact that] the world is becoming more global, and sharing health problems and solutions may serve as the future of understanding and dissecting the complexities of health care.

Other researchers have also noticed a characteristic concern for others—evidence of an equity ethic—in URM students, from undergraduates to postdoctoral researchers. Kenneth Gibbs and Kimberly Griffin studied postdoctoral biomedical scientists from both non-URM and URM backgrounds.[3] The non-URM scientists often cited freedom to choose their own research topics as a main reason to pursue a faculty career, whereas URM postdoctoral scholars were more often driven by goals such as mentoring students like themselves and addressing health problems in their communities. In addition, Dustin Thoman and colleagues discovered that, compared to White students, more URM undergraduates in all disciplines expressed altruistic work goals, such as jobs that offer the chance to help others. These students' wish to help others coexisted with other goals of having interesting and well-paid work, which are often top motivators for scientists.[4]

Another group of researchers observed URM science trainees at the Northeast Scientific Training Programs Retreat and found that many

wanted their traditional scientific research to have a social justice component: "This desire appears to reflect the sense of disconnect and marginalization that trainees feel within the academy and the scientific
community. It also appears to align with their concerns for issues such
as health disparities, which are evident for underrepresented/disadvan-
taged groups."[5] And in a study of six thousand undergraduates, Juan
Garibay found that equity, social justice, helping others through their
work, and working for social change were more important to URM
STEM students than to their non-URM peers.[6]

For some of my Black and Latinx study participants, an area of special concern was products aimed at people with dark skin and African hair. Kami, a Black chemistry and math major, was concerned that
dark-skinned African and Indian people are persuaded to use products
that bleach their skin so as to conform to beauty standards that do not
include them and thus to gain social acceptance. She hoped to become
a cosmetics chemist and start a business:

> My dream job would be to own [a] skin and hair care company. I
> see a lot of make-up lines and stuff that cater towards Africans and
> African Americans, but those companies hire very few Black chemists
> and cosmetologists. I want to help people feel beautiful about their
> natural Black selves. My friends go to MAC [a popular makeup line],
> and they are very dark, and it's hard to find those colors that fit them.
> Or even for African hair in general, it's so hard—every time you turn
> around, there's something else that you should try, and most of it is
> ruining our hair.[7]

ROOTS OF THE EQUITY ETHIC:
A COMMON HISTORY OF SUFFERING

The history of Africans in America began with suffering. From the kid-
napping and enslavement of Africans to contemporary racism, America

has created a culture and a common history of traumatization that continues today. Enslavement was followed by segregation, Jim Crow, denial of citizenship rights (voting and speech), redlining, and being barred from good schooling because students are educated by zip code. Lynching—public execution by mobs for often imagined crimes—was used to terrorize and control the Black population. Indigenous people also have a long history of suffering at the hands of settlers and the US government: eviction from their native lands (e.g., the Trail of Tears), massacres, and being shunted to reservations where educational, social, health, and health care disparities are persistent challenges to their well-being. Many Latinx people or their ancestors have come from impoverished countries and have systemically remained poor in the United States, living in segregated areas and working low-wage service and agricultural jobs.

Shared misery and exclusion from mainstream society can lead to the cultivation of helping behaviors, according to several scholars.[8] Marginalized people who get into college and achieve academic success often feel responsible for younger and older generations, which translates into engineering their skills or positions to advocate for social change. Generally, they want to give others the benefit of their STEM experience in empathic and caring ways. This can involve mentoring other students, talking to their communities about the career paths available to them, and integrating equity-based work into their STEM pursuits.

URM STUDENTS' COMPASSION AND THEIR FOCUS ON PRACTICAL SOLUTIONS

URM students have overwhelmingly expressed a keen desire to work for racial and global justice. They want to remedy inequalities they might have witnessed or experienced firsthand. This tendency is reflected in choice of occupation, with many Black college students, for example,

choosing careers in social work, civil rights law, and nonprofit organizations because they feel obligated to help others in need.[9]

Latasha was an African American chemistry major in her junior year.
She was already serving as a mentor to first-year students in the sciences, passing on invaluable resources and her own knowledge of STEM
and life so they could avoid making the mistakes she had. A Black electrical engineering major, Elise, did not see herself staying in the field
indefinitely. She hoped eventually to mentor and teach "right here in
my community, especially in mathematics, because that's where a lot
of people struggle."[10]

The Black and Latina women I interviewed were often more involved
than the men in activities pertaining to racial and global justice during
their education, but their male counterparts also expressed an equity
ethic. Eduardo, a Latino male, told me about the Neglected Diseases
Institute and its regional offices in various parts of the world. He hoped
to deploy a master's degree in bioengineering to address disparities in
health care. He looked forward to combining engineering, chemistry,
and biology to reduce the incidence of treatable diseases around the
world with better and cheaper vaccines and medicines:

> This may sound weird, but I would love to work in Third World coun-
> tries and tackle diseases like dysentery, malaria, leukemia, I think,
> and TB . . . I want to track the disease in real time with real people
> that I can watch heal. I really felt more closely related to neglected
> diseases; a neglected disease is poverty—it can be cured. But just a lot
> of the time there's not the resources there or the kind of people to
> devote to it.[11]

FAMILY, FICTIVE KINSHIP, AND COMMUNITY

Cultural values differ, and family definition is often broader among
URM people than in mainstream White communities. In Black, Latinx,

and Indigenous cultures, the individual is often less important than the family or the group, whereas mainstream Euro American culture is more individualistic. For instance, almost all the undergraduates in one study of Black STEM students' motivation named their families as external sources of motivation.[12] In my 2017 study of URM undergrads in STEM, most of my participants hoped that their example would inspire relatives to excel and explicitly urged them to complete their education and training. Nineteen of forty-four Black engineering PhD hopefuls in another study also cited family as a strong motivation for completing the degree.[13] In Christopher Jett and Julius Davis's survey of Black male STEM students, respondents recognized how much strong family support structures had contributed to their success over the years.[14] They cited extended as well as immediate family members who offered tutoring, helped them develop their understanding of STEM topics, and advocated for their access to specialized academic programs.

Students who depend on their families for support often want to give back directly. About one-third of my URM study participants spoke of planning to use their heightened earning power to improve the lives of family members. Other researchers have found the same thing. When asked if there was anyone in his family he needed to provide for, one student in a study said:

> Well, it's not necessarily *have* to provide for, but it's definitely that I want to give back financially. My grandma, I'll definitely want her to be freer from the financial strings of her husband, and my mom, I'll get her right. And then, as far as my brothers, I'm going to help them out, but they're grown men . . . I can scoop them up a little bit, give them a boost.[15]

Providing financial support to family members who helped them get where they are and kept them on task is part of many URM students' future plans. Family members may have sacrificed, financially and otherwise, for these students, and so they often feel the responsibility to family is paramount. Also, their narratives counter the common stereotype that families of color are not involved in their children's academic lives. Several students became emotional when they spoke about the many sacrifices their family members made to support their STEM academic and career dreams.

Nonfamily social ties can also support academic success. Research done over several decades has shown that Black male students in constructed communities of like-minded individuals fare better than their more isolated peers.[16] They support one another to excel in STEM disciplines. Black men who meet as undergraduates sometimes forge bonds that can help to sustain them as they move into and through graduate school. Groups like these meet the definition of the anthropological concept of *fictive kinship*: a connection between people not related by blood or marriage who sustain a mutually beneficial social relationships, or a familial relationship with people who are not family.[17] Those who have been part of strong, mutually supportive groups of Black men in higher education may have formed these groups in response to failure to bond with White male students, who dominate their classes but who consciously or unconsciously exclude them.

Perhaps this is why one research group found that science and mathematics classes that took on a communal and kinship structure markedly increased student motivation at two HBCUs.[18] Using the collaborative learning communities instead of lectures resulted in students' becoming actively engaged in learning. URM students may benefit most from this kind of inquiry-based learning, in which students have a lot of personal interaction, share information, and learn collaboratively. Being actively engaged in learning lets students create, discover, and understand scientific concepts deeply. While working in groups, they collaborate. They weigh new ideas, think critically, and exercise responsibility toward one another, in the process becoming fluent in the tasks at hand.[19]

DISCOMFORT WITH SUPPORTING
US ECONOMIC DOMINATION

The prevailing perception of using STEM to dominate the world is a source of ambivalence about their choice of career for many URM STEM students, men and women. In the words of one Black student who had left an engineering major, quoted in Elaine Seymour and Nancy Hewitt's ethnographic study:

> A big concern of a lot of Black students is we feel like we're being prepared to go into white corporate America, and it won't really help our community—we won't have the opportunity through our careers to give back to the community. Anything that we do for the community would be outside of our academic field, and that's a very serious concern.[20]

Six of the students in my 2017 study also feared spending their lives in careers that pay well and garner recognition but would not allow them to contribute practically to solving the problems of humanity. Hector, a Latino mathematics major, is one of them:

> The American Dream is what we are taught. I mean, literally all my mentors have said to me, "Hey, go get a job; after 40 years or so you retire, and everybody's all happy like that." So my generation is just cranking, you know, and working this all the time, but maybe that's depressing. I want to do something that I actually enjoy. So if that means helping people and I have to take a little pay cut [so that I can help] real people with real issues . . . sometimes it's just worth it.[21]

TESTING THE STRENGTH OF MOTIVATION

Rigorous, sharply competitive, and replete with racial and gender stereotypes about who can succeed, doctoral engineering programs are especially tough on women and minoritized people.[22] It is not surprising, therefore, that as of 2016, Black people accounted for less than 2 percent of all PhD students in engineering fields. That year, six colleagues and I published a study of what motivates these rare students. We looked at the difficulty they have had in constructing and maintaining identity in a society and in a discipline that doubts their ability.[23] We wanted to know why they opted to study engineering and what might account for their being able to stick to it. We also examined the varying strengths of intrinsic and extrinsic motivators in an environment that discredits these students, looking for the strategies they used to cope.

We defined motivation as the psychological forces that determine behavior, the amount of effort one applies, and one's persistence in the face of difficulties. Our PhD study participants (twenty-five men, fifteen women; some of them postdoctoral researchers) faced plenty of difficulty in their engineering departments: racial microaggressions, open and veiled questioning of their skills and abilities, and a conspicuous lack of other Black engineering students. Our open-ended discussions revealed a variety of motivating factors. *Intrinsic motivation* refers to doing something because it is inherently rewarding, interesting, or challenging or because it offers a sense of accomplishment or a chance to achieve one's potential. *Extrinsic motivation* comes from outside the individual and often means rewards, such as praise, social recognition, or money. Avoiding something unpleasant is also an extrinsic motivator.

After analyzing our participant interviews, we broke down their intrinsic motivations for pursuing advanced engineering degrees into

TABLE 4.1

*Motivating factors identified in black engineering doctoral candidates
and postdoctoral researchers*

	Number of participants showing evidence of the motivator (N = 40)
Intrinsic motivators	
Desire to help others	29
Mentoring or role-modeling for underrepresented students	25
Strong interest in the field; curiosity; passion for engineering	22
Earning respect and autonomy	19
Extrinsic motivators	
Undergraduate academic mentorship	23
Encouragement from family and friends; prior engineering-centered work experiences	17
An excellent opportunity	16

Source: Ebony O. McGee et al., "Black Engineering Students' Motivation for PhD Attainment: Passion plus Purpose," *Journal for Multicultural Education 10,* no. 2 (2016): 167–193.

four categories and their extrinsic motivations into three categories (see table 4.1). By far, the greatest single motivator for these students was a desire to help others; almost 75 percent of participants wanted to use their degree to make a meaningful difference in the world. An equity ethic also underlaid the next most common motivation: twenty-five of the forty participants wanted to become academic role models for other URM students, thereby helping them achieve their full potential. This intrinsic motivation often grew out of their own experience, since more than half our respondents mentioned receiving help from mentors as a major reason for embarking on the PhD program. Other external motivating factors were finding an opportunity that was too good to pass up, which sometimes included funding, and general posi-tive encouragement from family and friends.

The fact that many students had benefited from good mentoring motivated them to pay it forward and mentor other students like them-selves. One third-year postdoctoral engineer credited a single mentor with his decision to go after a doctorate:

> My PhD advisor probably is the singular reason I actually decided to get a PhD. I met him at the beginning of my senior year . . . I became really fascinated with the work he was doing . . . He is great at really instilling confidence in what you can do and he really believes in creating a more diverse academic world and really believes in the idea of bringing underrepresented people into the world of academia.[24]

Several students anticipated that earning the doctorate would finally silence those who doubt their ability and put an end to the stress of discrimination on the basis of race. One participant who was just start-ing a doctoral program in computer science said: "If there's anything I look forward to, it's how I can have a team of, like, all these guys that think, 'Are you sure you know what you know?' and I'm, like, 'Yup, I know it, and I'm your boss, so.'"[25] However, when the stereotypes and racial microaggressions do not stop—and I have not spoken with one URM STEM faculty member who does not still experience discrimina-tion at work—their personal equity ethic may serve as an omnipresent motivator for their persistence.

HOW TO ATTRACT AND RETAIN
UNDERREPRESENTED PEOPLE IN STEM FIELDS
Encourage the Equity Ethic

An obvious way to interest URM students with an equity ethic in pur-suing STEM careers is to design curricula that give them the chance to apply their skills to humanitarian projects and products in concert with the discipline. Several programs are doing this already, such as Youth Radio Interactive in Berkeley, California.[26] This division of Youth Radio allows young people to collaborate with professional designers and developers to construct mobile applications, games, maps, online quizzes, and other digital content. They learn to write computer code on critical, culturally relevant issues, such as the mental health struggles of urban youth of color, sexual assault in schools, gentrification, and the experiences of LGBTQ+ youth. The program uses "a learning ecology that values and leverages the prior knowledge, experiences, and backgrounds of our youth, while fostering the rigorous skills necessary to produce high-quality media that reaches audiences in the tens of millions" through outlets like Google Play, NPR, the *Atlantic*, and *Teen Vogue*.[27]

A pedagogical approach that has been used effectively in engineering education is community service learning, in which college students work with younger students. According to Michelle Camacho and Susan Lord, who studied the experience of Latinas in engineering, doing this kind of peer mentoring seems to foster a greater feeling of belonging in college for Latinx students.[28] This mutually beneficial mentoring process could be especially useful for universities located near communities with large Latinx populations.

Camacho and Lord also cited a first-year engineering class at the University of Colorado that gave students the chance to do hands-on work. It exposed them to design principles, encouraged personal relationships between students on small teams, and concentrated on real-world projects such as low-tech solutions to problems in developing countries. This novel approach to teaching engineering concepts helped to increase retention of women students in the program by 27 percent and Latinx students by 54 percent.

Establish Learning Communities
for Students and Faculty

A learning community is an educational approach that emphasizes interpersonal interaction, collaborative learning, and sharing information. This type of collaborative pedagogy grew from theories on active, inquiry-based learning as well as newer modes of instruction that appeal to diverse learners. It has turned out to be an especially valuable way to teach science because it leads to deep conceptual understanding, which sets up a solid base for further learning. And, as Kimberly Freeman, Sharon Alston, and Duvon Winborne point out, "African Americans may benefit the most from these types of innovative pedagogies."[29] This group of researchers studied the nature and level of student interest, attitudes, learning experiences, and motivation in STEM as they took specially designed science classes at two HBCUs. They found that students were intellectually enriched by encountering materials and tasks that they had to tackle as a team. The design of the classes compelled them to consider other perspectives and ideas, be responsible to one another, and engage in critical thinking together. In contrast to traditional lectures that enforce passivity, the students' active engagement allowed them to recreate the scientific process in class, which led to deep understanding of the material.

Offer Culturally Affirming Content

Culturally responsive teaching recognizes, affirms, and values students' culture and their unique experiences. Acknowledging the importance and the strengths of nonmainstream cultures can have an outsized effect. Camacho and Lord explored culturally responsive teaching for Latinx cultures, which requires instructors to acknowledge their students' various identities and to establish a safe community in their classrooms.[30] Many URM cultures value a holistic process of establishing context and prior knowledge before trying to solve a problem. This culturally responsive teaching process is not typical of university instruction, but seeing a problem from several perspectives should be viewed as an effective way to teach all students.

The special tribulations of Black men in STEM. Black men are often viewed pathologically in US society, framed as dangerous, hostile, and incompetent. A reimagination of Black male presence in society and education is long overdue, as several researchers contend.[31] Culturally responsive and racial justice–oriented instructional practices can be used to support Black males in STEM.[32] Being culturally responsive involves building on Black men's nonschool STEM experiences and rich familial and community STEM practices—playing card games, dominoes, or dice; braiding hair; taking public transportation—which can be used to catalyze their learning in all STEM disciplines. These instructional practices include having students write STEM autobiographies; complete racial justice projects using STEM principles to address problems affecting Black males, their families, and their communities; and conduct research on past and present Black STEM professionals.[33] Culturally affirming teaching practices employ Black men's community knowledge to teach STEM content that addresses social issues and advances justice on those issues.

Practices such as these can affirm, empower, and transform Black male students' STEM identities, leading to greater STEM success.[34] For example, Terry engaged a team of Black male high school students in culturally relevant and racial justice mathematical tasks like those listed above.[35] To develop critical mathematics literacies, they analyzed mathematical data related to rates of college graduation, homicide, and incarceration among Black males in the students' own community and nationally. Extending these practices to college-level STEM instruction could have further benefits.

Researchers Jett and Davis recommend similar professional learning and development sessions for STEM faculty, instructional leaders,
and administrators.[36] Support for development of instructional materials from this perspective is also necessary. Future work should include
measures to determine how Black males think, reason, and make sense
of STEM in an interdisciplinary way, drawing from STEM organizations
and task forces that encourage problem-based, applied STEM teaching,
learning, and research in an empowering way. It should also draw on
the growing body of research on Black manhood to engage Black males
in teaching and learning in STEM disciplines.[37]

Intersectional issues: Women of color in STEM. Ashley, a Black second-
year materials science student, had decided against an academic career
because it conflicted with her equity ethic, concluding that "teaching
is not really an emphasis for tenure-track professors." In other words,
the academic area that she and many other URM students were most
attracted to was often the least valued by institutions, whereas con-
ducting research, publishing research, and getting research grants are
of primary worth. As she said, "[M]ost minorities come from a very
community-based and a familial background, [so] that cutthroat and
no-real-care-for-other-people-if-it-doesn't-directly-benefit-you [mental-
ity is] . . . I think that's one of the reasons that they don't go into academia." Forsaking an academic career, Ashley took a job in industry,
developing prosthetics and thereby increasing equity for people with
physical disabilities.[38]

As women faculty in the physical sciences went from 16 percent of
the total in 2001 to 24 percent in 2013, faculty participation rates for
Black women have been stuck at 2 percent, even though Black women
have been earning a larger percentage of doctoral degrees every year.[39]
More broadly, URM women faculty in all disciplines earn tenure at the
lowest rate of all groups.[40] These statistics reflect the stark reality of the

double bind for women of color in STEM, which has different effects than either race or gender discrimination by itself. This double bind, or intersectionality effect (which acknowledges that racism intersects with other forms of oppression such as gender, sexuality, or disability status for URM people), puts women of color in STEM in a position of exaggerated social isolation and alienation from their disciplines. The National Science Foundation has begun to address problems of intersectionality through its ADVANCE Institutional Transformation (IT) grant program.[41] Researchers Mary Armstrong and Jasna Jovanovic found that diversity leaders and administrators of these grants at four-teen US institutions of higher education were using the IT grants to fund programs such as external mentoring (matching mentees of a particular ethnic or racial minority and gender with mentors of the same group outside the institution), focus groups, and other efforts to meet URM women's needs; to keep them in their degree programs; and to facilitate retention, tenure, and promotion for URM women STEM faculty.

The researchers sought commonalities in programs that appeared to be working. Although most of these intersectional IT grant efforts focused on helping individual faculty members over specific hurdles, Armstrong and Jovanovic identified several efforts targeted at chang-ing the overall institutional climate to support URM women. These included *creating accountable leaders* (e.g., senior administrators who understand intersectional issues and enforce consequences for those who ignore those issues); *identifying climate zones*, or being aware that different climates exist within an institution (e.g., colleges, depart-ments, labs), each of which may require a different strategy; *setting up programs for microclimates* caused by different types of bias for Latinas and Black women; *training majority faculty to become effective allies* for URM women; and *promoting structures* that bring URM women together, create community, and let them define their needs. The researchers suggest that the most effective use of IT grants could simultaneously deploy, say, a group entry strategy (recruiting and hiring several URM women at one time), setting up institutionwide workshops on bias against URM women modifying interview processes to allow job candidates to meet with URM women faculty, and running a lecture series on diversity in STEM. Less effective use of the IT grants employed an additive approach, which focused on women and minoritized groups separately and tended to blur distinctions between White women and URM women.[42]

Another group studied the phenomenon of URM women in STEM creating physical and conceptual counterspaces (or brave spaces) for mutual support. To combat the problem of not feeling like they belong in STEM spaces, the women they interviewed made use of counterspaces in peer-to-peer relationships, national conferences on diversity in STEM, campus groups (both STEM and non-STEM), mentoring relationships, and even STEM departments in which races and genders mixed and racism was not tolerated. These brave spaces allowed them to share their work and private lives, validate their experiences, maintain a collegial race- and gender-based climate, and do things like invite women scientists to speak. STEM departments that functioned as counterspaces offered tuition-free precollege programs for URM women students, hosted diversity support programs, and paid for students to attend conferences, especially diversity conferences, that they could not afford. As the women shared their experiences in a sheltered atmosphere, they could see their personal encounters with discrimination and stereotyping as reflections of the systemic racism in their department or institution.[43]

Some of these nontoxic spaces included majority-female classes in STEM subjects. One Latina professional in physics spoke of her small, upper-level undergraduate physics class that was almost all women—a rarity at her HWI:

[The impact on me] was huge, because all of a sudden, we could ask questions . . . [If] there are more women out there, if I say something wrong, it's okay. It's really okay. And it is okay because for one, obviously, I am not the only woman here, so I'm not assigned to carry the flag of females in physics.[44]

CHAPTER FIVE

Evaluating Efforts
to Broaden
STEM Participation

SOME THREE DECADES AGO, strategies for bringing more people of color into STEM education were proposed, including federal and private funding for programs with a record of producing scientific talent, partnerships between institutions that serve URMs and research-intensive universities, initiatives for minority-serving institutions, and a tenure process that rewards the mentoring of URMs.[1] Some of these recommended initiatives came into being, but they have had little effect on the number of URM students in STEM fields or on their level of comfort and acceptance there. That happened because many of these initiatives were founded on an incomplete understanding of why some groups remain underrepresented in STEM fields. So URM students and faculty still enter a system full of discriminatory barriers that are known to harm their health and well-being while racialized bias and beliefs about their incompetence continue.[2] The burden rests on the URM STEM community to prove their worth to a skeptical majority and to assimilate as best they can into the dominant, Eurocentric culture; that is, a culture that derives from a system based on White, male, heterosexual, Christian, able-bodied, middle- to upper-class values.[3]

In this chapter, I discuss the best methods of integrating URM students into American STEM departments, but I want to be clear: most of these approaches try to fix the student while leaving the fundamentally exclusionary racist structures intact. Overall, as the dismal retention rates for URM students and faculty demonstrate, these attempts at increasing diversity are not working. In his book on the hidden racist principles of American universities, Craig Wilder draws attention to the ways that slavery, patriarchal authority, and philosophies about racial difference were present at the founding of many US institutions of higher education and are still very much alive: "Universities that . . . position themselves as idealized sites of diversity and inclusion are often complicit in global systems of racialized capitalism, and buttressed by oppressive histories that maintain their economic health and political capital."[4]

I argue that US universities, especially their STEM departments, are due for some courageous self-examination and radical overhaul. It is time to acknowledge that the practice of science is impoverished by its lack of diverse points of view. The scientific goal of objectivity is more likely to result from including the opinions, perspectives, and histories of people of color that have been excluded for so long.

EFFECTIVE EDUCATIONAL APPROACHES FOR UNDERREPRESENTED STUDENTS IN STEM

To increase the probability of an equitable educational experience for all students interested in STEM disciplines, I recommend several broad principles based on the research of many education scholars.[5] Researchers have found that it is most effective to create a faculty community and institutional environment that welcomes all students, to acknowledge and value the cultural differences of URM students, and to socialize them into the academic discipline through research and meaningful interactions with faculty. Institutional policies should ensure that all students have access to all programs and can bring the richness of their identities to their schooling rather than suppressing aspects of themselves in attempts to fit in. Also necessary are true reform of curriculum and methods of instruction as well as greater financial support for students who need it most.

Many students, both URM and otherwise, have faulted the quality of instruction in scientific and technical fields. In interviews with African American and Latinx students who had 600 or better SAT mathematics scores but chose nonscience majors, students most often cited teachers' attitudes, behavior, and teaching ability as the primary factors in their choice of major. They saw science, mathematics, and engineering teachers as "arrogant, unavailable, or unapproachable," whereas those in other disciplines were not only more caring and encouraging, they conveyed their subject matter more effectively.[6] In a 1997 study of 335 undergraduates, some 90 percent of those who abandoned STEM disciplines and 74 percent of those who persisted in STEM described the teaching in STEM subjects as poor; quality of instruction was a major factor in the decision to switch from a STEM major.[7] Other researchers found that a strongly student-oriented faculty made undergraduate biology students more likely to stay in science and pursue research careers than did a strongly research-oriented faculty (perhaps because they relied more on teaching assistants).[8]

The following three sections describe the types of interventions undertaken at majority-White universities that have proved to be most successful at raising the number of URM students in STEM disciplines and increasing their satisfaction there.

Create a Welcoming Environment

- *Start a learning center.* Many institutions of higher education operate learning centers to boost student performance and retention and to develop teaching skills. The Mathematics and Science Learning Center at Rutgers University, for instance, hosts interactive exhibits, course materials, a study area and library, a computer lab, mini-labs in biology and physics, instructional videotapes (e.g., on problem solving), and instructor-led group tutoring and review sessions. It currently draws at least 85,000 student visits annually.[9]

- *Offer workshops and seminars in study skills, exploring careers, and test preparation.* URM undergraduates who are thinking of graduate school benefit considerably from workshops that familiarize students with test content and structure and reduce test anxiety. Since faculty often train graduates student to become faculty members, workshops in nonacademic STEM PhD careers would offer expanded career trajectories.[10]

- *Emphasize career counseling and awareness and financial support.* It is likely that most people know a physician or a dentist, but fewer people have met a scientist, engineer, or mathematician—and meeting such professionals is a major determinant of Black students' persistence in science-based disciplines. Even high-achieving URM students demonstrate scant knowledge of the full range of careers available to them. Financial aid is also critical for students from low–socioeconomic status backgrounds, as many URM students are. A study by the US General Accounting Office found that, for students from the poorest families, moving as little as $1,000 from scholarship to loan made these students 17 percent *less* likely to graduate college.[11]

- *Increase the quantity and quality of academic advising,* including orientation to the institution, in order to improve graduation rates. Researchers confirmed that staff advisers can be as effective as faculty advisers and that Black students greatly preferred individual counseling to group counseling. Especially helpful are training programs for student advisers that promote the development of meaningful student-teacher interactions. Another valuable area in which to concentrate institutional efforts is establishing a system that ensures a regular flow of information to students about their academic progress.[12]

Focus Holistically on Students' STEM Growth

Education researchers have repeatedly found that involving under-graduate STEM students in research increases their chances of staying in a STEM discipline, perhaps because it is a key aspect of socializing students into a scientific or technological discipline. One study found that, compared to similar alumni with no research experience, those who had taken part in a university's undergraduate research program were significantly more satisfied with their education and were more likely to attend and complete graduate school.[13] In addition, taking part in research leads to attending conferences, presenting work at conferences, and publishing research, all of which are important factors in students' development of professional self-confidence. Socializing students into a profession also boosts their self-efficacy, which is a major predictor of good grades and persistence in STEM majors.[14]

Reform Curriculum and Instruction

The way STEM subjects are taught in the United States is ripe for remodeling. In one study, high-achieving recent college graduates reported that "the physical sciences are presented in too narrow a teaching and learning mode" and there was "little opportunity to use the skills they learn elsewhere, particularly their verbal skills, in making sense of the material."[15]

Two promising pedagogical approaches especially suited to technical disciplines are expanding the design and teamwork aspects of instruction and involving students in more hands-on work. Increasing engineering classes' focus on design, teamwork, hands-on projects, and real-world problems has proved to be especially effective for Latinx students and women, in one case boosting retention of Latinx engineering students by more than 50 percent and women engineering students by 27 percent.[16] Active participation in design teams or lab groups balances the comparatively passive lecture format. In science and engineering disciplines, expanding the instructional focus on establishing prior knowledge and creating context capitalizes on the social aspects of many Latinx cultures; these are also necessary steps in problem solving, a foundational skill for engineering and other STEM disciplines. These instructional methods are aspects of *culturally responsive teaching*, which also requires instructors to recognize each student's identity and make the classroom an affirming space in which students can publicly test their understanding.[17]

Observers have found that *community service learning*, in which college students work with younger students in communities of color that resemble their own, has proven merit for both Black and Latinx groups and correlates with an increased sense of belonging in college for these groups.[18] These innovative approaches to instruction create a more engaging environment that is especially effective for URM students.

In another study describing a redesigned calculus sequence, changes included active learning, creative use of lecturing and other pedagogical methods, and increased student-faculty contact. A greater use of group projects and workshop sessions resulted in higher average grades and retention than in a comparison group enrolled in the standard calculus course. The more engaging environment appeared to be the critical component leading to better student outcomes.[19]

PROGRAMS THAT WORK
FOR STEM STUDENTS OF COLOR

Jasmine, a Black engineering major, told me about her experience in a bridge program designed for URM students the summer before she started college. The Engineering and Science Success Academy benefited her on several levels:

It got me more acquainted with what college would be like . . . We had a really rigorous schedule. We had recitations from . . . 6:30 p.m. to like 10 p.m. We took college classes, but they weren't for credit. The whole program was like two credits . . . [I]t was really like a family, because everybody we had met through that program, we continued to see throughout the school year. It helped me feel more included, so I didn't feel so alone when I got here.

Prefreshman bridge programs ease the transition to the culture and expectations of college life, and participants are more likely than nonparticipants to persist in college. These programs combat the isolation and culture shock that newly arrived URM students can encounter in college while introducing them to collegiate standards and skills. Classes can include mathematics, reading, composition, study skills, and word processing. Some bridge programs incorporate tutoring, academic and career counseling, and mentoring that continues through the following academic year.[20] According to analysts at the Meyerhoff Scholars Program, these preparatory programs have contributed significantly to student success.[21] In this section, I review several effective programs for students of color in STEM.

Meyerhoff Scholars Program

Begun in 1989 to increase the number of Black male STEM PhD holders, the Meyerhoff Scholars Program at University of Maryland Baltimore County (UMBC) now enrolls largely URM students who excel in math and science and builds their knowledge, skills, and motivation in an emotionally supportive environment. They start with a summer bridge program, after which they receive four-year scholarships contingent on performance. Services include monitoring academic progress, advising and mentoring, study groups, tutoring, and summer research internships. As of this writing, there are more than a thousand

Meyerhoff alumni, 76 percent of whom have earned graduate or professional degrees.[22]

The program's success has sparked two Meyerhoff replicates. In 2013, the University of North Carolina Chapel Hill and Pennsylvania State University worked closely with Meyerhoff staff to set up the Chancellor's Science Scholars Program (UNC) and the Millennium Scholars Program (Penn State). Their first five years have seen success rates similar to or better than UMBC's. Two key factors in their success appear to be the use of all the Meyerhoff elements, not just a select few, and keeping the cohort size reasonable. As the director of the UNC program said, when the cohorts grow too large, "you start to really have a negative impact on cohort dynamics and you don't get the type of cohesion that you would like to see in a group." In 2019, two University of California schools, Berkeley and San Diego, announced plans to replicate the model in partnership with UMBC.[23]

Minority Engineering Program

The first Minority Engineering Program (MEP), started in 1973 by Ray Landis, a California State University professor, has been copied at more than a hundred universities and private programs. In two early MEPs, students remained in the field of engineering at higher rates than did the entire group of engineering students on the campuses where they operated.[24] By 1994, the MEP at California State University at Sacramento had a retention rate of 80 percent.[25] Results for all MEPs are mixed, but one pair of researchers found that the eight most successful MEPs did the following: recruited at the high school level, offered summer programs in content knowledge and critical thinking, had strong faculty support and institutional funding, provided study centers, and had enough tutors for all the students.[26]

Mathematics Workshop Program

Another highly effective and widely copied program for URM scholars is the Mathematics Workshop Program, developed by Dr. Uri Treisman at the University of California, Berkeley. Its purpose was to increase the numbers of African American and Latinx students who entered the university interested in careers in math, science, or engineering to persist to degree completion. The program's core techniques are the use of problem sets that compel group interaction and the creation of a safe place in which students can verbalize their understanding as it develops. It emphasizes group learning, efficient studying, and a community whose members share an interest in mathematics. Students who enroll in the Mathematics Workshop Program and many of its imitators have gotten higher grades, repeated courses at lower rates, taken more-advanced math courses, and selected and stayed in STEM majors at higher rates compared to nonparticipants. Notably, the program's Black and Latinx participants have earned better grades than all their nonparticipant URM, White, and Asian classmates.[27]

It is clear that the types of interventions that work for URM students—student-centered learning, innovative curricula, group learning, joining in faculty-led research, high-quality advising, tutoring, and internships—can also work for all students. STEM departments reap many positive gains from programs that help their URM students do well in these disciplines, including higher graduation rates and increased student satisfaction with their education, but the effects can be broader and deeper. For one, UMBC has seen a dramatic uptick in faculty attitudes toward Black students' scientific abilities and performance after introduction of the Meyerhoff initiative to the campus.[28] As this model program is copied elsewhere, we can hope for similar changes to local faculty members' viewpoints on the abilities of URM students. And if faculty members' attitudes can change, we can hope that non-URM students' attitudes will also shift and eventually students of color in STEM will be less of a novelty.

GUIDING PRINCIPLES
OF URM STUDENT PROGRAMS

A leading light in the process of productive interference in URM student education is Dr. Robbin Chapman of Harvard University's Kennedy School. Some of the same principles that propel the success of students in the three programs just reviewed are evident in her Thrive Mosaic Scholar Framework. According to Chapman, the best way for URM students to establish ownership of their professional growth in biased arenas is to create a mosaic of various types of allies. As Chapman said, these allies offer students "access to often invisible information and opportunities not available to URM scholars. The Thrive Mosaic is intended to increase redistribution of community cultural wealth, academic capital, and social capital within privileged and exclusive academic spaces."[29]

One ally a young scholar should identify is an *associate*, such as another student, who will be a partner for accountability, mutual support, and becoming aware of and taking control of one's learning. Associates trade status updates, focus on meeting deadlines, formulate action steps to meet goals, troubleshoot, and celebrate milestones. *Advocates* are academics or professionals who can talk about the students' work, write letters of support, nominate students for awards or leadership opportunities, and help them get appointments or assignments. A student can have several *mentors* to guide them in the discipline's culture; some mentors address a student's general progress toward a career, while others focus on a particular area, such as developing grants. Advocates and mentors might not share the student's race or ethnic background but must acknowledge their unconscious biases related to race or other identities and work to minimize their negative effects (cross-cultural competence). Coaches, targeted trainers, and connectors round out the field of those who can help young URM scholars through the years of study and the early years of academic and professional positions.

Chapman's framework and the three programs just described surround URM students with protective structures and people to build and maintain students' skills and confidence in predominantly White educational spaces. They harness the power of groups. Whether it's a series of allies who guide and provide critical information (Chapman) or a cohort of peers who build a learning culture together (like Jasmine's "family" in the section opener), these various structures function to prevent URM students from becoming academically and socially isolated. Breaking new ground can be lonely, and all these interventions formalize support from sympathetic, knowledgeable, and sometimes powerful people. Other commonalities are respect for students' intellectual capacity, which the math and engineering programs reflect in their multipronged approach of tutoring, study groups, and student-centered learning. The Thrive Mosaic Framework demonstrates this respect by encouraging young scholars to seek advocates and associates with whom to discuss their work and coaches and targeted trainers to help with specific subjects.

All these academic interventions are aimed at building a critical mass of URM students, scholars, academics, and professionals throughout the many STEM fields, which will inspire greater numbers of young URMs to reach for their dreams.

WHY IS MENTORING IMPORTANT?

In a 2015 survey of Black, Mexican American, and Puerto Rican faculty by Ruth Zambrana and colleagues, many participants described experiences like that of this Mexican American professor, who lamented his lack of mentoring when he needed it most:

> To get through that [Ivy League undergraduate] experience . . . it was a moment of true cultural, education, language, socioeconomic, religious shock of my life. Those first two years in college . . . were the most difficult part of my entire educational training of the 18 years [after high school]. [In comparison,] I found [graduate school] not difficult at all.[30]

Other study participants who did receive good mentoring at the right times said that it made it possible for them to stay in college and to graduate. Their mentors gave them emotional support, accountability, the skills and strategies they needed to negotiate higher education, and a way of understanding themselves in relation to race- and class-based systems of inequality. Without mentoring that mediated the gulf between their socioeconomic backgrounds and the privileged world of higher education, many URM participants said they probably would have either changed their major to anything but STEM—or worse, dropped out of higher education completely.

Mentoring is crucial to URM students' degree completion; one study found that it was the most important factor in Latinx students' finishing a degree program, and another found it was one of the top-two key factors for Indigenous students.[31] However, URM students receive mentoring less often than White students do.[32]

Racial stereotyping pervades URM students' relationships with White and Asian STEM faculty. Some faculty members regard URM students as poorly prepared, not committed to research, lacking in "passion" (often a euphemism for intellectual incompetence), and having low aspirations. None of these attitudes should characterize prospective mentors of URM students. Beliefs like these impede high-quality mentoring and disrupt the necessary process of professional socialization.[33]

Several researchers studied Black mentee–White mentor pairings and found that mentors with color-blind attitudes (i.e., professing belief that race is unimportant) stifled any frank discussion of race, thereby impairing the trust that underlies mentoring relationships.[34] These mentors may fear that taking any notice of race will mark them as racist, but this attitude actually makes their mentoring ineffective.

Mentoring that is informed by racial or multicultural competence offers protection for URM graduate students who want to carry out non-Eurocentric centered research. Mentors who do not acknowledge or respect cultural differences tend to discourage graduate students and junior faculty from research on issues of oppression and racism, sometimes claiming that they are not worthy of scholarly attention or are not a proper subject for scientific study. Other mentors might steer mentees away from such subject matter in an effort to shield URM graduate students from the judgment of less "woke" colleagues.[35] Whatever the reasoning might be, the deracializing of URM graduate students' research can feel like attempts at forced cultural assimilation to people whose very reason for pursuing an advanced degree might be to tackle issues in marginalized communities. Advisers and mentors who do not understand or accept a student's research interests can increase the student's self-doubt, intellectual isolation, and distrust of the institution.[36] Other effects include the perpetuation of racist structures and attitudes in higher education.[37]

Many aspects of effective mentoring are well known, but this gathering of the latest research on mentoring in the following sections uniquely sums up what constitutes the best mentoring available for URM students.

A CAUTION ABOUT
MENTORING PROGRAMMING

Mentoring is not a cure-all, and even the best mentoring outcomes have their limits against institutions and departments that have deeply embedded racialized practices, behaviors, and policies. Thus, each department is a mini-institution, with its own microculture, values, and ideologies, and thus it can address engrained racialized and other types of bias that have contributed to the ineffective mentoring of URM students and kept them from thriving in the field. Some mentoring initiatives have reflected ideologies similar to neoliberalism, which often reduces its programming to calculations of wealth and productivity. Research has demonstrated that some conceptualizations of Black resilience derived from the civil rights movement (e.g., celebrating Black people's inherent strength and will to overcome structural racism) but have been altered to glorify personal resilience and resourcefulness, which thereby downplays or eliminates the responsibility of departments and institutions to help students maintain STEM resilience. Neoliberal mentoring practices reveal how racial empowerment, uplift, or resilience mentoring initiatives are contrived and oversimplified representations of URMs' experience and a way of masking structural racism and hegemony.[38]

To believe that attainments as complex as success, happiness, love, and meaning can be attributed to a short list of personal traits such as virtue, faith, perseverance, self-control, grit, and positive thinking is inspiring but naive.[39] The fact is that students who get the resources they require for success in their STEM environments are far more likely to succeed than individuals with positive thoughts and memorable quotes from the latest TED Talk. STEM mentoring programs focused on URM students should be guided by critical theories that challenge deficit-based perceptions mentors may have of their protégés. Program leaders should question and counter the minoritization of people of color and their forced adaptation to dominant ideology.

MENTORING FOR THE UNDERREPRESENTED AND MINORITIZED

Underrepresented graduate and undergraduate students in STEM fields will derive the greatest benefit from mentoring programs that do all the following:

- Provide respectful, significant relationships with mentors who both support and challenge them
- Value mentees' intellect and knowledge
- Develop and reinforce mentees' scientific identity (or mathematical, technology professional, or engineering identity)
- Offer institutional support, such as financial aid
- Involve mentees in research, including opportunities to guide them through research design, execution, and analysis
- Offer affective support in ways such as acknowledging the struggle of URM groups, supporting mentees' interest in racial justice issues, and helping mentees identify and talk about oppression
- Enable support from faculty, peers (e.g., advanced students of the same ethnic group), and staff
- Provide role models in the form of URM and/or women faculty
- Review the unwritten rules and expectations of the institution's dominant culture without condescension or requiring mentees to erase their own culture[40]

In virtually all US institutions of higher education, but especially in research-intensive universities, cross-racial mentoring of STEM students of color will be unavoidable. Most mentoring for women STEM students will be cross-gender. In all probability, LGBTQ+ people and those who have different levels of ableness must also make do with mentors who do not resemble them, although a 2017 National Science Foundation study concluded that one in nine scientists and engineers has some sort of disability. In order to mentor URM students competently, faculty members from dominant groups must acknowledge the existence of unequal power relationships, discrimination, stereotyping, and oppression of URM groups. For that to happen, education and training are in order, but the good news is that it can be done: White mentors who have done successful cross-race mentoring developed new awareness of the challenges URM students face, and they came to know and understand their mentees as individuals by learning their students' personal histories and goals.[41]

As detailed in the Thrive Mosaic Framework discussed earlier, students can benefit greatly from having multiple mentors at various times in their educational careers. Different types of mentors offer different things to mentees, and peers as well as industry professionals can also be tapped for some mentoring duties. To combat the isolation URM STEM students often experience, the relatively new option of e-mentoring can offer support and advice from mentors they may never meet in person. One e-mentoring network is MentorNet, which sets up yearlong mentoring associations between URM and women STEM students and professionals in academia and industry. Another source of e-mentoring is a website I cofounded, BlackengineeringPhD, which offers a variety of mentoring supports for Black engineering doctoral students. The newly established Institute in Critical Quantitative, Computational, & Mixed Methodologies (ICQCM, found at http://criticalscholars4quantresearch.org/) is a training institute that I cofounded for scholars from underrepresented backgrounds and scholars doing critical research on communities of color. Our mission is to advance the presence of scholars of color among those using data science methodologies and to challenge researchers to use those methods in ways that can dismantle the structural barriers to enable humanity, equity, and justice for underrepresented communities, professionals, and young people.

Early-career URM faculty require many of the elements listed above for good graduate and undergraduate mentoring, as well as the following:

- political guidance, in the form of learning academic norms, strategies, and skills that increase mentees' influence while protecting their research ideas and goals
- inclusion in major grant proposals and coauthoring opportunities
- hands-on critique and revision of their thinking and writing (i.e., modeling scholarly writing) as they formulate arguments and articulate ideas
- creation of a local URM faculty community with senior URM faculty and administrators
- honoring the connection between mentees' service to their communities and their research
- challenging institutional politics and power relations on behalf of mentees[42]

Some Less-Obvious Benefits of Mentoring

One sign of successful mentoring is a mentee's interest in "paying it forward" by becoming a mentor to others, whether they are fellow students, junior faculty members, or middle school students who are interested in STEM subjects. This practice is common among Latinx and Black college students, and URM faculty members often feel so responsible for mentoring other URMs that their own careers suffer as a result.

White faculty who engage in cross-race mentoring can benefit from expansion of their networks as their mentees advance in their careers and from getting help carrying out their own research. Personal rewards can include a sense of altruism, feeling capable, enjoying their mentees' achievements, and having their own horizons expanded, with positive repercussions for their own research.[43]

CLEARING THE PATHWAY
TO DIVERSIFIED STEM EXCELLENCE

Mentoring is a key aspect of many programs devoted to the advancement of URM students. Other components (e.g., stipends, research and internship opportunities, attending conferences, and presenting research) increase students' self-efficacy in their academic domain and help to build their discipline-specific social identities. A social identity is built on a set of norms, attitudes, traits, and stereotypes that form a prototype, or ideal group member.[44] Those who deviate from the prototype are marginalized and not extended full membership in the group. Anyone who aspires to join a STEM field but is not White, male, heterosexual, able-bodied, middle class or higher, or historically not seen as a scientist does not receive the full benefits and opportunities that more prototypical group members receive. Students underrepresented by race and/or gender have often been expected to conform to the dominant White male culture or a prescribed stereotypical role of what qualities and characteristics a women scientist should embody.[45] Keeping their social and academic peer networks separate and downplaying their racial and/or gendered identities forces URM STEM students to compartmentalize themselves instead of integrating these critical personal identities into their science identities.[46]

As the chief diversity officer of Diversity Policy and Programs at the Association of American Medical Colleges, Dr. Marcus Nivet published a penetrating commentary on the slow pace of diversity in higher education, with a special focus on medical schools.[47] In his view, diversifying higher education must be seen as more than just solving the problem of inadequate representation or recruiting students and faculty to achieve population parity. Diversifying higher education means breaking down the barriers facing disadvantaged and marginalized populations, and it must be tightly coupled with developing a culture of inclusion that fully appreciates different perspectives; in other words, diversity is a pathway to excellence. Retaining URM students and employees should therefore be at the heart of the academic mission and not merely a matter of compliance with government mandates. The task of diversifying higher education, especially STEM education, will require diversity of thought, expression, desires, and goals, and will ultimately enhance the experience of all students, faculty, and staff. It will move diversity from the periphery of academic life to the core of institutional culture.

CHAPTER SIX

Next Steps for
STEM Leadership

Practical Suggestions for Structural Change

LET ME BE VERY CLEAR: the entirety of STEM higher education needs to be dismantled, period. Then, with people of color (POC) within and beyond STEM leading the effort, the whole STEM instructional and workforce system should be redesigned to be equitable and inclusive, with the goals of celebrating racial diversity and innovation in STEM. This must include a radical critique of the applications of scientific knowledge and disassembly of the dominant ways of thinking about how science and technology are done. In a magnificent article, Helen Zhao affirms the need for these radical actions:

> This kind of critique brings to light the many, often horrifying, ways in which technological and ideological results of knowledge production abet and reinforce ruling-class power, domination, and exploitation of workers and the oppressed. It makes clear the devastating knock-on effects of science on society, such as napalm, nuclear bombs, forced sterilization, hate crimes, unjust social policies, racist criminal risk algorithms, [and] facial recognition scanners at border checkpoints.[1]

By-products of this transformation will include culturally affirming and responsive STEM enterprise that is likely to serve justice, which is good for our society and our planet. But while we STEM warriors are preparing for this structural battle—and I doubt it will happen just because it's the right thing to do—here are some good-faith steps that universities can take to prepare for the STEM revolution.

It's safe to say that POC have not in any significant way contributed to the human development that is causing climate change, otherwise known as environmental capitalism. After all, no underrepresented POC in the United States own airlines or aircraft manufacturers, which generate 3.4 percent of carbon dioxide emissions as of 2018, thus making air travel and shipping the world's largest single source of emissions for the third year in a row.[2] We don't own large technology companies such as Apple, Google, and Microsoft, whose workplace environments are full of racism, sexism, racialized bullying, sexual harassment, and stereotyping.[3]

We did not design and do not run large social media or digital streaming companies, such as Facebook, Netflix, and Twitter. A former Facebook manager admitted that the company has a "black people problem."[4] Facebook has been investigated for complicity in Russian interference in the 2016 presidential election. The resulting Trump presidency has unraveled decades of climate-protecting policies as he opens up wilderness areas and national parks to resource exploitation. Trump has refused to sign an international agreement to protect the rapidly melting Arctic region unless it was stripped of any references to climate change, which is having worldwide effects.[5] As I write this chapter, both the Arctic and the Amazon rainforest (which produces a significant percentage of earth's oxygen) are on fire.[6]

We POC also do not own a single automobile manufacturer, whose products collectively account for nearly one-fifth of *all* US greenhouse-gas emissions and whose management is behind the opposition to urban public transportation projects, which disproportionally affect communities of color.[7] Furthermore, POC are not responsible for the racial disparities in auto insurance, mortgage loans, DNA crime evidence, and facial recognition—even artificial intelligence machines are learning to be racist.[8]

So why are POC some of the biggest consumers of computing and technology innovations when they play virtually no role in the ownership and leadership of technology companies? Why do well-publicized diversity campaigns and outreach efforts by STEM industries' largest companies and trade groups position employment in their firms, rather than pathways to ownership, as the diversity goal for underrepresented POC? What role do these companies play in (un)intentionally blocking POC's pathway from STEM education to STEM employment? Why has the percentage of POC employed in the largest computing and technology firms increased only slightly at most companies and decreased slightly at others, despite their well-publicized outreach efforts? My attempt to answer these questions took me deep into the foundation and structures of STEM, looking particularly at how racism operates in the experiences, ideologies, practices, and policies of STEM training programs. This historical structural analysis departs from many analyses of the lack of racial diversity in STEM graduate education and employment, which is generally explained using the pipeline analogy (i.e., too few racially diverse people in STEM education leads to too little diversity in STEM industry).[9]

THE POWER OF THE UNIVERSITY

This is what POC are bringing and continue to bring to STEM; in return, this is what the university can and should do to support them better.

What Black, Latinx, and Indigenous cultures can offer STEM disciplines— and vice versa. Studies show that human evolution has predisposed us to share tasks, goods, and services, and much of this human sharing is governed by social norms of fairness and equity.[10] Thus, the human species has succeeded in part because of traits like compassion and working collaboratively, which suggests that cooperation is more fundamental to the optimal functioning of human society than competition.[11]

Black, Indigenous, and Latinx cultures have long embraced a strong sense of kinship within their own racial groups, and this kinship is sometimes extended to other minoritized groups of color. They also have a shared cultural identity in the pursuit of common goals (e.g., civil rights, tribal rights, equitable learning spaces), along with a sense of interdependence and group-mindedness.[12] Black, Indigenous, and Latinx cultures are likely to experience oppression and discrimination and to recognize inequity and social suffering in similarly situated groups. Unlike personal suffering, which is unrelated to social identity, *social suffering* refers to a group's suffering "which inspires a collective imagination of a 'we' who suffer."[13] Those who recognize their collective suffering as structural can develop social empathy with their own groups and with other oppressed minorities; this process leads to developing a contextual understanding of inequity and feeling responsible to effect change.[14]

Thus, the way STEM industry and education have been designed and developed is not in sync with our history of surviving through collaborating, understanding, and adapting to each other, through working together and distributing our gains equitably. The culture of virtually every STEM discipline reeks of vicious competition, intellectual elitism, racialized hierarchies of ability, and gross inequalities. No wonder, then, that POC who are trying to learn and practice in these fields are frequently alienated and dissatisfied. If STEM culture embraced the values and cultures of POC, just imagine how cooperative, unique, and innovative STEM products and outcomes would be.

There is a long and sordid history of Black STEM intellectuals being left out of the STEM enterprise. One of the first Black scholars to publish on the role of race and racism in STEM education in the United States was Black historian Carter G. Woodson. Woodson provided strong evidence that race and racism are prevalent in most aspects of Black Americans' lives and that the education systems to which they have access are particularly inequitable. Woodson's major thesis was that Black Americans have been educated away from their culture and traditions and toward European values and traditions, which is psychologically damaging for them.[15] Woodson proclaimed, "Even in the certitude of science and mathematics it has been unfortunate that the approach to the Negro has been borrowed from a 'foreign [Eurocentric] method.'"[16]

For years, Black scholars and educators have worked to bring out the best in Black students in spite of the widespread presumption of White intellectual superiority. Dr. Robert P. Moses, a Black mathematics scholar and founder of the Algebra Project, is a premiere example of people who have recognized the importance of mathematical skills for Black people and sought ways to develop Black students' mathematical understanding. Beginning with the 1960s civil rights movement, he demonstrated that those who are mathematically competent are better positioned than those who are not to reduce the structural barriers that lead to economic dependence, and thus they have more opportunities to increase their autonomy and self-determination.[17] Moses and his coauthor urgently argued that mathematics literacy is the key to the future of the disenfranchised communities in which Black Americans disproportionately reside. They claimed that numeracy was a new civil rights issue because mathematics in general and algebra specifically act as curricular gatekeepers; significant opportunity opens up both educationally and economically for those who succeed in this content area.

Another leader in this area is S. E. Anderson, a founding member of the Black Panther Party and a current activist, teacher, and writer. Anderson has taught mathematics, science, and Black history at the college level. He predicted in 1970 that "liberation" would be part of any serious analysis of Black intellectual thought in STEM.[18] The following quote encompasses some of his thinking about Blacks in STEM, as he suggests that Black people "should learn mathematics not because American capitalism's advanced forms of technology require this background, but because Black Liberation Struggle against the American racist-capitalist system requires [this] knowledge."[19] Anderson's work contrasts with traditional schools of thought that valorize STEM careers and celebrate the mere visual representation of Black and Brown bodies in the STEM system, while privately despising and sabotaging the efforts of underrepresented STEM scholars. Anderson noted that, as an identifiable group to be exploited, Black scientists, economists, architects, technicians, engineers, and doctors are a by-product of an oppressive capitalistic system.[20]

Regarding Latinx students, I must bring up the resurgence of nativism, that is, recent overt hostility toward certain racial groups, which is heightened when marginalized peoples and immigrants fall into identifiable racial categories that are familiar to the American psyche (e.g., Latinx-sounding last names, "accents," style of dress).[21] Latinx peoples have historically been the target of racism and nativism that affects their access to equitable education, among other things. Latinxs have enjoyed higher rates of college STEM enrollment and graduation in comparison to their Black and Indigenous peers, even when we examine these numbers proportionally. Scholars who study Latinxs in STEM have posited that assimilation tactics have been pushed on Latinx students as the key to demonstrating cultural orientation to Americanized values and STEM success.[22] In recent years, some Latinx leaders have proposed that adopting American values, culture, and language will allow Latinx assimilation, as happened with White European immigrants in the early twentieth century.[23] However, other scholars suggest that, as immigrants spend time in the United States, they become more aware of their discriminatory status. They form an *ethnic resilience perspective* that leads to ethnic consciousness and provides the foundation for interpreting negative experiences in terms of discrimination.[24] This perspective causes them to resist assimilation and to recognize that the idea of meritocracy is not real. However, in this racist educational climate, the Republican-leaning US Supreme Court surprisingly ruled in favor of the nearly seven hundred thousand Deferred Action for Childhood Arrivals (DACA). Notably, the US Supreme Court's ruling does not prevent the Trump administration from trying again, thus Latinx STEM students, teachers, and professors are still at risk.

Tactics, strategies, or even ideologies employed by Latinx students and faculty, whether that be assimilation, adopting an ethnic resilience perspective, or something else, are no match for the racist policies, laws, and practices being enforced. Even the best strategy is likely to be ineffective against policies and laws that enforce racism. Also, access to financial assistance, which is critical for the persistence of Latinx students in STEM, may be hampered by governmental policies that restrict access to Latinx immigrant students.[25] Not to mention that the Trump administration's executive orders on Latinx immigrants have cost American taxpayers about $70 billion.[26] That's $70 billion for enforcement, detention facilities, immigration judges, and transportation in a system that has harmed immigrants' mental and physical health and led to the deaths of at least seven children. I wonder what would have become of those seven children if they had had an opportunity to thrive in the United States, and maybe even in STEM.

Focusing on the recruitment and retention of Latinx people in STEM is generally seen as an important thing to do because their numbers are increasing: the Latinx population is projected to be 26.8 percent of the total in 2050.[27] The Trump administration's policies will limit their full, authentic participation in STEM, but if we want the largest population of color, nearly one-third of the nation, to buy STEM products and services, it makes great business sense to include them in the design, development, execution, and implementation of STEM innovation. In this book, I have stressed that we need current and future scientists who look like the world we are serving in order to truly advance innovation. Here is another message: don't mess up your money by having only White folx at the table. Ignoring or disserving a huge segment of the populace can only hurt a company's bottom line.

Now I come to the Indigenous part of the US population, who barely show up in STEM participation statistics. In an attempt to counter the four-hundred-year history of mistreatment and devaluing of the people who were here long before Europeans arrived, I offer a few observations. This one comes from a pair of researchers who view Indigenous groups as holders of a valuable, overlooked body of knowledge that we need now:

> Indigenous peoples throughout the world have sustained their unique world views and associated knowledge systems for millennia . . . The depth of Indigenous knowledge rooted in the long inhabitation of a particular place offers lessons that can benefit everyone, from educator to scientist, as we search for a more satisfying and sustainable way to live on this planet.[28]

Those charged with educating Indigenous students, particularly in STEM subjects, would do well to consider the knowledge these students already possess or have access to. Their forebears did not survive extreme environments such as tundra and high desert without advanced expertise in weather, climate, animal behavior, astronomy, and mathematics. One cofounder of an organization called Future Indigenous Educators suggests that a mathematics teacher could use the shapes in Navajo rugs to teach principles of geometry: "There's meaning behind those designs. There are names for each of them. The thought process, the mathematical thinking that rug weavers may have that we [educators] really don't know about is in there."[29]

Indigenous people had to know the natural world deeply and intimately in order to keep themselves alive for thousands of years. Gathering wild foods and hunting was a sustainable way of life for millions of humans. In contrast, a few centuries of European agriculture, with its row crops and livestock, has degraded this nation's once-rich soils and polluted our water and air. Agricultural scientists respond to low soil fertility and increased susceptibility to insects by inventing new fertilizers, pesticides, and herbicides and splicing genes into staple grains in hopes of keeping the agribusiness model going, but these marginally effective solutions seem increasingly desperate. Far from being a fad, the move toward sustainability in energy and agriculture looks more and more like the only way forward. Pockets of research in STEM disciplines focus on sustainability, and Indigenous people know a lot about that.

Those who have studied Indigenous knowledge recognize that these preliterate peoples knew things that Western science has only recently discovered:

> Through long observation they [Indigenous peoples] have become specialists in understanding the interconnectedness and holism of our place in the universe . . . The new sciences of chaos and complexity and the study of nonlinear dynamic systems have helped Western scientists also to recognize order in phenomena that were previously considered chaotic and random. These patterns reveal less visible sets of relationships that point to the essential balances and diversity that help nature thrive. Indigenous people have long recognized these interdependencies and have sought to maintain harmony with all of life.[30]

Complex knowledge like this was critical to their survival, and it is still passed down in the form of stories. Even now, it is not unusual for elders to tell stories to children for two or three hours at a time, in a structured form of repetition that could also include songs and visual art.[31] Some of these ancient stories convey geological information that jibes with current understanding. The Blackfoot people of the Northwest Plains, for example, have a cache of origin stories about Naapi, a personification of the forces that shaped the earth. Sometimes called Old Man or Trickster, Naapi is "a recognized personage or Being who created the world."[32] In one Naapi creation story, this larger-than-life figure moved chunks of the landscape around, "pushing himself through when he got stuck between two mountains," thereby creating valleys in the Rocky Mountains. Other stories refer to some of Naapi's "resting places" above the ice sheets that once covered the Blackfoot homeland. Researchers have located ancient camp circles on these hilltops that date back to the Ice Age, thereby confirming the content of these stories.

A way of life that was so close to the land also shaped Indigenous people's ways of learning. One researcher watched children while living among the Ojibwe:

> Ojibwe children . . . are taught skills of active watching and listening, not simply the content of what to look or listen for. They are taught to take in cultural lessons experientially, to take them in over time, and to not expect spoon feedings of segmented units of knowledge.[33]

STEM teachers of Indigenous students can honor the observational skills of their forebears in various ways, including cultivating curiosity. Being curious about the world is characteristic of all children—and is the fundamental scientific quality—but schools often discourage that, especially in this era of standardized testing.[34] Educating Indigenous students should be a two-way transaction that reinforces the knowledge of their ancestors and respects their abilities.[35]

Why universities need POC on their campuses to thrive. Universities are the places where great creativity, innovation, and technological feats take place. Universities have a high concentration of talented teachers, researchers, and students who thrive in an environment that fosters collaboration, scientific inquiry, critical thinking, innovation, and creativity. Institutions can sometimes become more agile by carefully balancing the number of externally imposed standards to manage their resources efficiently and respond quickly to the demands of a rapidly changing global market.

Universities can also help to embolden White nationalism and other racist ideologies.[36] White supremacist activities are spreading rapidly across campuses, fueled by the current political and social climate. Some elite universities, such as Princeton, Harvard, Columbia, MIT, Brown, Georgetown, and the University of Virginia, have acknowledged their role in the perpetuation of slavery and their part in the sordid history of ill-gotten wealth from slave trading and slavery.[37] Although Harvard and Georgetown are having reparations discussions, votes, and dialogue, they have yet to pay reparations, with the exception of an endowment set up for descendants of enslaved Georgetown University workers (this does not address what it owes to descendants who have already completed university degrees).[38]

The following seven practical steps for increasing inclusion of URM students will harness the power and agility of universities to increase URM students' graduation rates as well as their comfort, safety, and health. Institutions that do not address their lack of students of color will cease to grow as the US population becomes increasingly diverse in the coming decades.

Hire More Faculty of Color in STEM Faculty Positions

Sparked by national Black student protests in 2015 and 2016, Black faculty at more than eighty institutions wrote, "WE DEMAND at the minimum, Black students and Black faculty [should] be reflected by the national percentage of Black folk in the country" (emphasis original).[39] However, in spite of several prominent colleges and universities promising to increase the racial diversity of their faculty, the actual percentage of Black faculty has fallen slightly, from 7 percent in 2006 to 6.6 percent in 2016, and the 6.6 percent includes a small number of nonfaculty employee hires.[40] More racially minoritized faculty and staff must be advanced through tenure and promotion and put in senior roles, including administration. Indigenous STEM faculty, using Indigenous research methodology, can offer STEM fields a combination of native culture, language, self-determination, and a unique history to guide their research, with personal connections and higher levels of equity.[41]

Implement Identity-Conscious STEM Mentoring Programs

Although theories and research on mentoring relationships have grown, they continue to lag behind program development, implementation, and evaluation of mentoring at the local, state, and national levels. Academics characterize this area of research as underdeveloped. STEM mentoring programs need better guidelines to consider the dynamic intersections of students' social identities and STEM identities and discourage color-blind and assimilationist approaches for supporting URM student retention. Faculty of color pay a high price for being mentors and are often overloaded by the high number of students they mentor. Helping URM students navigate academic culture, deal with personal or family problems, or find resources to keep them in college takes an emotional toll. Research shows that universities did not value

URM faculty mentoring and that it disproportionately hurt the careers of URM faculty by taking time away from research and publications.[42]

Providing training and professional development to faculty members—especially those who lack adequate mentoring experience, skills, and/or credentials—can make mentorship a critical component of graduate education. Training and coaching on mentoring will help improve both formal and informal mentoring relationships. Recognizing the time-intensive nature of mentoring and its associated workload, institutional leaders should reward this critical aspect of education through compensation, tenure, and promotion; this important step could shift the institutional culture toward working for greater diversity. Since being a faculty member does not automatically endow one with mentoring skills, it is necessary to provide professional development and mentoring support for all faculty. When all faculty members are able to engage in holistic mentoring practices with URM STEM students, all STEM students will ultimately benefit.

Hire Counselors of Color Who Specialize in the Trauma Experienced by STEM Higher Education Students (and Faculty)

While university counseling centers have been experiencing a recent surge in students utilizing these resources, for a variety of reasons (the most important being insufficient racially diverse counselors and additional fees for some services), many students of color do not receive counseling that could help to offset their racial trauma. STEM departments are places where racial stereotyping runs rampant and racial battle fatigue is common among URM students. The Association for University and College Counseling Center Directors reported an average student-to-counselor ratio of 1:1,411 from July 2017 to June 2018.[43] And with upward of $100 per visit for students, cost is a significant

barrier to well-being care for traumatized students of color who are trying to survive their often racist and sexist STEM environments.

Universities should be accountable for the experiences that contribute to racial battle fatigue in their very own STEM students of color.
They cannot create trauma for STEM students of color and then fail
to provide services for their well-being. Universities have the power to
adjust their policies and practices to slash fees, reduce wait times, and
promote racial diversity among campus counselors. This would mean
professional development training on the institutional culture of many
STEM departments as well as training for counselors that addresses the
racism and sexism that cause mental health trauma. For example, the
University of Maryland College Park Counseling Center established
special days or times for students of color to speak to counselors of
color; this makes the entire counseling center experience and programming a more welcoming environment. The University of Kentucky
is one institution that has established mechanisms to report bias.[44]
Beyond that, however, the principle of eliminating or at least reducing bias should hold faculty, administrators, staff, and fellow students
accountable for reducing their own bias through training and possibly
sanctions for multiple offenders.

Create Pathways for People of Color to Pursue STEM Entrepreneurship

I am not equating entrepreneurship with liberation for STEMers of
color. I am not naive enough to think that we can solve racial inequities in STEM with a POC-owned social media firm, aerospace company,
or new Black Microsoft. The wealth gap (White households are thirteen
times as wealthy as Black households), the poisoning of Black babies
(they breathe polluted air, drink poisoned water, and live in leaded
houses at higher rates than other racial groups), mass incarceration
(there were 1,549 Black prisoners for every 100,000 Black adults in the

United States—nearly six times the imprisonment rate for Whites), double-digit unemployment (Black college graduates have the same chance of getting a job as a White person with less education), redlining (homes in Black neighborhoods are valued, on average, $48,000 less than homes in White neighborhoods with similar crime rates and amenities)—all this can hardly be blamed on the dearth of Black STEM entrepreneurship.[45] But I also know that entrepreneurship cannot hurt the standing of POC in STEM spaces either. Historically, inclusion initiatives have focused mostly on White women founders and rarely on those who are Black, Latinx, or Indigenous.

There is an ongoing nationwide effort to increase the number of POC engaged in entrepreneurship and innovation in STEM to meet the United States' growing workforce needs. In addition, there is a growing desire to diversify the STEM workforce to be more representative of the nation's population. However, in spite of these efforts, the country and the world as a whole continue to suffer from a lack of entrepreneurs and innovators of color. It is essential to understand the successes of POC, to eliminate the barriers to their entrepreneurship, and to provide innovative science and technology that will accommodate the needs of all people. POC entrepreneurs would bolster the discovery of innovative solutions to some of the world's toughest challenges, such as the National Academy of Engineering's Grand Challenges and the United Nations' sustainable development goals.[46] Although the advantages of engaging all citizens in innovation are broadly recognized, this country lags behind other nations in attracting underrepresented and marginalized people to pursue science and technology degrees and establish business enterprises. Providing more funding to transform and enhance these entrepreneurship education and accelerator programs (e.g., NSF I-Corps, Y Combinator, Techstars, VentureWell's E-Teams) would lead to more opportunities for POC in STEM. Role models like Joy Buolamwini, founder and CEO of Algorithmic Justice League; Danielle Forward,

founder of Natives Rising; Kathryn Finney, founder and CEO of digi-
talundivided; Brandeis Marshall, founder and CEO of DataedX and
Spelman College professor of computing; and Natalia Oberti Noguera,
founder and CEO of Pipeline Angels, all could provide consulting and
programming in support of these entrepreneurial efforts.

Retrain STEM Faculty and Industry Leaders

Those who lead industry and educational institutions and those who
teach need to acknowledge that their own STEM education is characterized by (1) the exclusion of non-Whites from positions of power,
which almost completely erases Indigenous theories and contributions
to STEM; (2) the development of a White frame that organizes STEM
ideologies and normalizes White racial superiority; (3) the historical
construction of a curricular model based on the thinking of White
elites, thus disregarding all the cultures that contributed to STEM globally; and (4) the assertion of knowledge and knowledge production as
neutral, objective, and unconnected to power relations.[47] STEM education and occupations were designed to attract White men who are
heterosexual, able-bodied, slim, Christian or atheist, middle-class and
above, and, more recently, certain Asian groups designated as acceptable. Therefore, the curriculum and products of this culture contribute
to an inhospitable environment for students, faculty, and employees
who do not fit these criteria. Exposing STEM faculty and industry leaders to books such as *The Crest of the Peacock: Non-European Roots of Mathematics* would spread the word that humans all over the planet, not just
White Europeans, are capable of advanced and innovative STEM thinking and invention.[48] A related reference is *Blacks in Science: Ancient and
Modern*, a compilation of thoroughly researched papers that document
Africa's contributions to astronomy, agriculture, architecture, engineering, aeronautics, mathematics, medicine, metallurgy, physics, and writing systems.[49] Current STEM faculty members would greatly benefit

from participating in antiracism professional development training that discusses definitions of power, White privilege, White supremacy, global anti-Blackness, the model minority myth, institutional racism, race and class barriers, and internalized oppression.[50]

Acknowledge the Work of STEM Research Educators

STEM faculty members instruct on how mathematics and natural sciences are used in research, development, design, manufacturing, systems, or technical operations in order to create systems, products, processes, and services of a technical nature.[51] STEM research programs were designed to produce graduates with a measure of knowledge and character who could take on roles in industry; the focus was highly pragmatic. Divergently, STEM research educators perform research on the interplay of STEM with the larger elements of human society. This complex interface between STEM and the contexts in which it is embedded—racial, intellectual, economic, and more—define both the educational approaches taken and how various approaches are valued. While the evolution of racist practice and ideas can affect STEM, so too does STEM affect the marketing and reproduction of racist practices in science and technology. This is where STEM education researchers can make a significant impact on understanding and dismantling the racist and sexist structures of many STEM environments.

In the last twenty years or so, Black, Latinx, and Indigenous STEM education researchers, mostly led by the critical mathematics education community, have been offering jewels of wisdom for transforming our STEM environments, both academic and industrial, into learning spaces that are more racially equitable and that acknowledge the brilliance of POC in STEM. They include scholars and activists such as Jomo Mutegi, Rochelle Gutierrez, Nicole Joseph, Bob Moses, Aisha Bowe, Julian Davis, Kimberly Bryant, Chris Jett, Aprille Ericsson, Danny Martin, Jedidah Isler, William Tate, Chanda Prescod-Weinstein, Robert

Berry, Crystal Hill Morton, Lamont Terry, Erica Walker, James Moore III, Luis Ponjuan, Monica Cox, Gregory Larnell, Maisie Gholson, Luis Leyva, Jackie Leonard, Erika Bullock, Eileen Parsons, Estela Mara Bensimon, Bevlee Watford, Brooke Coley, Julia Aguirre, and Kathy Deer-InWater. They challenge and critique the mainstream discourse and treatment of POC in STEM, with the aim of transforming conditions and improving racial equity in the larger STEM community, especially women of color and other marginalized groups.

These STEM education researchers clap back against the technological and ideological uses of science and technology to impair, oppress, colonize, and exclude people from political and scientific power. They call for revolutionizing the gendered, raced, heteronormative material bases of STEM: the funding bodies, institutional cultures and structures, and publication editors who uphold White supremacist standards.[52] Intellectual thought in STEM by these scholars and others entails inclusion of the theories and critical perspectives of major research positions and concepts put forth by minoritized people in relation to STEM. This multifaceted philosophy encompasses theory, epistemology, and existentialism; curriculum design; pedagogy; research approaches; the purposes of STEM for POC; and the forms and functions of STEM in relation to their lives. STEM education researcher scholars concerned with racial justice in STEM have long articulated the need to consider the broader social and structural constraints that foster limited racially diverse representation in STEM fields, which impedes progress, representation, and achievement in STEM.

Respect and Properly Fund HBCUs, HSIs, and Tribal Colleges as the Leaders of URM STEM Student Success

The cultural authority of institutions that educate STEM URMs is currently undervalued in national discussions of increasing diversity in STEM. These institutions have a legacy of liberatory leadership and empowerment to inspire, envision, and transform STEM climates to produce awe-inspiring numbers of URM university graduates.[53] The negative and incomplete depictions of these institutions, in both media and scholarly literature, have shifted them from the center of the national undergraduate STEM enterprise to the margins. Collectively, deficit-born perspectives on HBCUs, HSIs, and tribal colleges give rise to a problematic narrative that ignores the influence of URM STEM leadership in setting an institutional tone for broadening participation in these fields. If institutions are truly to be vessels for inspirational change and to apply their own power and privilege to produce knowledge, then we need STEM academic leaders who are willing to learn, convey, and act to prepare institutions for more diverse and inclusive approaches to STEM research.[54] We need look no further than the leaders of HBCUs, for example, who are ideally suited to preserving an institutional tone that recognizes, desires, fosters, and requires the actions and outcomes that are necessary for inclusion in STEM higher education.[55] Historically and currently, HBCUs have significantly outpaced all other institutions of higher education in graduating Black STEM students.[56] The expertise of HBCUs, HSIs, and tribal colleges could lead to more robust understanding of how the strategic use of limited symbolic, structural, political, and human resources can shape a URM STEM student's experience with a race-conscious environment that feeds broadening participation in STEM. These URM-serving institutions had to build their own ladders to STEM success for POC; it would be wise to take them seriously because they can reveal the unwritten codes that allow them to do so much more than other institutions (e.g., HWIs and private institutions) to broaden participation in STEM.

The blueprint is here for the rest of the STEM community to follow. It shows us how to integrate our unique personal and academic histories into an all-encompassing leadership practice that invites, with intentionality and specificity, positive outcomes from STEM broadening participation. The STEM community must concentrate on undoing the damage done by research that arises from privileged, exclusionary viewpoints. This means redoing research and reconsidering methods, lines of inquiry, and conceptualizing of problems in the context of inclusion.[57]

CONCLUSION

Power concedes nothing without a demand, and usually a fight. As I and others fight for structural changes and prepare for more institutional dismantling and rebuilding, these proposed practical steps for transforming and diversifying STEM education will help repair STEM environments in the meantime. Discriminatory structural barriers in STEM hamper our ability to cultivate talent, which is directly tied to understanding ways to promote the full inclusion of excellence across the racial spectrum. When we consider the problem solving required to create STEM breakthroughs, *diversity becomes key to excellence*. There is even a well-executed mathematical rationale and logic for diversity.[58] Thus, from the perspective of enlightened self-interest, it is best to recognize that the people and institutions who succeed in the twenty-first century and beyond will be those who have worked to educate themselves and acknowledge that diverse experiences, perspectives, and backgrounds are crucial to the development of new ideas, which makes the embracing of diversity a business and innovation imperative.

I leave you with recommendations from scholars who propose ways to remedy the lack of research on race, culture, and social stratification; social justice in education; the positive personal and academic development of URMs though an acknowledgment of multiple forms of discrimination; the formation and maintenance of mathematical and racial identities; processes of racial socialization; and race and gender intersectionality.

Recommendations for the STEM Community

Members of the STEM community must self-examine to look closely at their accepted belief systems and their existing diversity models and evaluate how well these are working. Studies of social-organizational climates might facilitate this type of investigation. Examining these climate data by age, ethnicity or race, gender, and STEM specialty can show areas that are ripe for diversity training and development. In addition, exit surveys of those who have left graduate programs or professional roles may yield data that reveal how personnel turnover shows evidence of entrenched ideological differences and expectations.[59]

Besides training related to instilling anti-racist practices in their research, advising, and teaching, STEM graduate programs and businesses should evaluate how their human resource systems, which are tools for STEM socialization, perpetuate diversity models that actually decrease the number of URMs in an organization. One important step is committing to difficult conversations on what applicants learn about an organization during site visits and about the ways an organization chooses and promotes talent reveal its diversity and inclusion values.

Recommendations for STEM Departments

STEM departments should consider how color-blind liberalism operates in their departments, focusing on areas such as distribution of resources to faculty and students, pedagogy, and policies affecting recruitment, admissions, hiring, and retention. STEM department leaders should contemplate the additional steps necessary for the department to develop, extend, and sustain equity-centered practices. Using the information collected, they can then construct an action plan that deals with the racialized experiences of students, faculty, and staff in the department.[60] All leaders, from the departmental level up, should work to increase their cultural competency and use their learning to inform programs, initiatives, and decisions. They should require that demonstrated cultural competency be part of all employees' promotion, merit, and performance reviews. A campuswide proactive bias-response plan should be set up to address both individual and institutional bias. University leaders are well positioned to start consortia through which many institutions can share information, resources, and implementation practices that address systemic historical barriers to URM scholars. These consortia can store evidence that will inform and guide their efforts. Leaders should also audit departmental and administrative units to track and measure progress toward minimizing bias in their operations.[61]

Recommendations for Policy Makers

Equitable teaching practices and scholar development in higher education should be promoted through policy. Current policies can be audited and reexamined regularly for inherent institutional bias and actions taken to address any bias uncovered. Policy makers can advocate policies that collect data and advance data assessment and information sharing for programs aimed at equitable access, advocacy, and professional development for STEM scholars throughout their careers. They can create portals where this information can be accessed for research. Policy makers can also work with the six regional accrediting agencies (e.g., US Department of Education, Council for Higher Education Accreditation) that hold universities accountable for maintaining quality standards to enact policy that mandates tackling of institutional bias issues as an accreditation quality standard.[62]

Who Am I to Be Writing a Book like This?

MY RESEARCH AND THUS THIS BOOK represent the convergence of three intersecting realms of my development trajectories—personal, professional, and scholarly development: (1) my personal experience as a mathematically striving Black woman; (2) my STEM research, teaching, and mentoring experience with racially minoritized students who exhibited academic and personal resilience but not without mental and physical health costs; and (3) my critical analysis of research on STEM learning and participation among racially minoritized students, faculty, administrators, and staff. My experience in these areas has convinced me of the need for rigorous research that extends our knowledge base and contributes to a fuller understanding of racially minoritized students in STEM. But let me start where it all started, with my mom.

I am the first to admit that it pays to have a high school mathematics teacher for a mother. Although my mom was my first mathematics teacher, she did not teach me much formal mathematics after kindergarten. Informal mathematics happened through her card game parties. Once a month, my mom or my great aunt and uncle would hold card game parties, where Black folk played Old Maid, tonk, bid whist, dominoes, spades, and checkers. They were a Black and beautiful synergy of Afrocentric culture and mathematics, laughter, joy, signifying, cussing, and hand gesturing. The spirit my Mama instilled in me was much greater than teaching academic mathematical concepts; I grew up not being afraid of or anxious about mathematics. I grew up witnessing

Black girls and women triumphing in mathematics—they won most of the card games when the Brothas weren't cheating—so even when the naysayers came for me, I could just go home and see Black women embodying mathematics. We lived on the South Side of Chicago, and contrary to popular opinion, opportunities for Black people to thrive were available, and my mother had an honorary PhD in looking out for her Black daughter.

Charlene (my mom) bought that monthly city bus pass and we took off: going to plays on the North Side, international children's films, festivals, and musical events. She even took me to lectures (maybe this is why I am a professor today). She made sure to nurture me holistically, but you best believe she put me in every mathematics summer camp, afterschool program, and special event that existed in Chicago, or at least it felt like that. She did it all while raising me on a substitute teacher's salary for the first eleven years of my life. When I turned twelve, my mom received her bachelor's degree in mathematics from Chicago State University; from that point on, I knew that I was going to prosper in a mathematics-based field.

In my teenage years, three major events happened that helped set me on my path toward being a doer of mathematics. First, in eighth grade, I tested into a preparatory high school. My mathematics skills were solid, but what I did not anticipate was how racism played out in this advanced academic environment. I had a downright racist mathematics teacher in my freshman year. At the end of that year, I had a 2.3 GPA and I felt defeated and deflated. I withdrew from the prep school and went to Corliss High School, where my mother taught. Corliss was a regular school in a Black neighborhood. It presented a stark difference from my multiracial, ultracompetitive prep school. Corliss had a reputation for poor academics that is stereotypical of underresourced high schools in Black communities, which were provided with insufficient resources by design. But I and many of my peers thrived; all my teachers believed in my abilities. In addition, I was expected to assume leadership positions in the school and the surrounding community. With my confidence up, Corliss gave me greater exposure to the treacherous plight associated with being Black in Chicago, and as you know, the challenges are great because structural racism has done a number on us. So, I joined Operation PUSH to get my racial justice activism on!

EARLY ACTIVISM AND THE
JACKIE ROBINSON FOUNDATION

The Rainbow PUSH Coalition grew out of the Southern Christian Leadership Conference's Operation Breadbasket, founded by Rev. Dr. Martin Luther King, Jr. The premise behind Operation Breadbasket was to demand material equity through securing employment at businesses whose services and products were marketed and sold to Black people. These businesses denied Black people jobs and/or advancement. Operation Breadbasket first attempted to negotiate more equitable employment practices with mostly White retail businesses and consumer-goods industries, including the hiring of Black employees. If negotiations did not yield positive and equitable employment outcomes, Operation Breadbasket boycotted and picketed those businesses until successful outcomes were delivered. (A comparable example today would be Black people boycotting Facebook because only 1 percent of Facebook's engineers and coders are Black.) In 1966, Dr. King appointed Jesse L. Jackson Sr. to serve as the first director of Operation Breadbasket in Chicago. In 1971, Jackson founded Operation PUSH (People United to Save Humanity) while he was a seminary student. I went there every Saturday and sometimes during the week. I helped the videographer, Lee Bush, videotape the Saturday morning sessions, which were a combination of social activism, church, and political commentary. I saw and heard the likes of Chicago aldermen, religious leaders, community activists, senators (yes, I do mean the man who would become President Barack Obama), Hollywood actors, and prominent Chicago businessmen. In my volunteer work with PUSH, I went to prisons on Christmas, fed the homeless, and helped with job training for the underemployed. I learned that both Jesse Jackson Sr. and Jr. attended North Carolina A&T State University, an HBCU that had a stellar reputation for teaching and graduating Blacks in engineering. I thought, "If it was good enough for them, it's good enough for me." And that was how I decided which college to attend.

The last major event of my high school years was receiving a Jackie Robinson Foundation (JRF) scholarship near the end of my senior year in high school. I was fortunate to receive a few scholarships, and for those funders I remain grateful, but the JRF had undertaken a specific mission for its money. For the final interview process, I remember being shuttled into a room with a panel of the most beautiful and polished Black people I had ever met in my life. To say I was nervous would be a gross understatement, but I channeled the voices of the speakers I'd heard at Operation PUSH and somehow I made it through. Originally, I was thrilled about getting financial support, but the JRF is so much more than that. Every year in March, all the JRF scholars and alumni were invited to the Jackie Robinson Scholarship weekend in New York City. We learned about financial planning, graduate school, and career options. We had lunch with our corporate sponsors, and the weekend culminated with a gala. Jackie Robinson's wife, Mrs. Rachel Robinson, the founder of JRF, was behind the scenes making it all happen.

Many JRF scholars were able to forge close relationships with Mrs. Robinson and her children, Sharon and David Robinson, who were also heavily involved with the JRF. Mrs. Robinson frequently led or co-led a very special session during the JRF weekend that left an undeniable impression on us JRF student scholars. We would create a circle with our chairs and share the most intimate stories of trauma we had experienced in college. That's when I learned firsthand about the almost omnipresent distress associated with being a high-achieving Black student on a White campus. We came to realize that no amount of top grades or coveted scholarships was powerful enough to dispel racialized stereotypes about our ability to succeed. During those sessions, I also discovered that there appeared to be an extra level of scrutiny associated with the Black JRF scholars majoring in STEM. They talked about getting hit from all sides—from their professors, their student peers, summer internship employers, deans, and other key stakeholders at their schools. It was during those sessions that I first realized that this heightened scrutiny had something to do with being Black and in STEM and that it went unreported, ignored, minimized, and as a result, normalized.

This realization was so traumatizing that the STEM JRF students began to get together on our own and share war stories about our experiences in college STEM. Most of us realized it was only during these sessions that we actually spoke the truth and, in some cases, finally told the truth to ourselves. This is because most people assumed that if you were a high-achieving student (i.e., with a high GPA and excellent test scores), you had no problems. A professor once told me, "You have a 3.9 GPA in electrical engineering and you're on full scholarship. What do you have to complain about? Your life is perfect." The students felt that complaining would characterize them as ungrateful or drama kings and queens. As a result, these students often took their racial abuse in silence.

The other message we often heard from our Black communities was the one about being resilient. Elders and other respected and successful people in our communities discussed their own hardships and how they used their internal drive to become successful. Thus, we heard a lot about pulling ourselves up by our bootstraps (even though not many Black folx use that exact language). We were coached to suck in our pain and take the racial abuse for the sake of our communities. Thus, the JRF became one of the few spaces where we could cry out loud, and without worrying about blowback. That's when I came to the conclusion that these STEM Black student scholars, who were mostly at HWIs, were all having the same debilitating experiences. But I wondered, instead of asking students to silently endure continuous racialized suffering, why weren't STEM departments and colleges taking responsibility for the pain and suffering? And why was it so easy for well-meaning Black folx (even our mothers and fathers, who love us more than anyone else in the world) to give us the impression that this was the price of university admission? They did not realize that this hardening of our racial armor could also lead to us fleeing STEM.

So, instead of focusing on the so-called pipeline as the heart of the problem of lack of diversity in STEM, we should pay more attention to the two-thirds of Black students who entered college with a STEM major and did not make it to the bachelor's degree. If programs were built to reverse this trend, would they include a race-conscious understanding of the ways in which STEM departments neglect the racial mental health of their students? It was through the JRF that I first contemplated these questions, and for better or worse, I'm still asking them.

COLLEGE YEARS AND MY FIRST ENGINEERING WORK

If I could name the five best decisions of my life, hands down, attending North Carolina A&T State University (NCAT) is definitely one of them (Aggie pride!). Yes, NCAT had all the woes of a typical southern Black university: long, hella long lines for everything; outdated dorm rooms; the computer lab equipment always on the fritz; and the cafeteria food—oh my God! But in retrospect, the benefits of attending NCAT were obvious from my first days there.

When I arrived on campus in fall of 1991 to start freshman year, I was told there was no campus housing for me. My mom gave me money to stay at a hotel for a couple of days, but that ran out fast. I'm not quite sure how it happened, but I was having dinner with Dr. Lonnie Sharpe, dean of the engineering school, and his wife and two younger brothers. We ate and chatted happily, and then he showed me to my room. Dr. and Mrs. Sharpe said something like, "You are going to stay in our house until your housing situation is resolved." This was my first time ever living in a house. The house was beautiful, and the Sharpes were beautiful. I stayed there at least two weeks longer than I was supposed to because I so enjoyed living in that house with that family. When I retell this story, particularly to my colleagues who attended other HBCUs, they often say, "This could only happen at an HBCU."

For this Chicago girl, the biggest culture shock of attending NCAT was not university life itself, it was living in the South. Luckily, NCAT gave me all the community I could ever desire: great friendships, productive and noncompetitive study groups, sorority pledging (oooooop!), coveted summer internships (e.g., General Electric, Ford Motor Company, NASA's Jet Propulsion Laboratory), and more. As an engineering major, I interacted with hundreds of bright, skillful, creative, future Black scientists, technologists, engineers, and mathematicians. Some of my teachers looked like me, and they believed in the potential of their Black students, both in STEM fields and in life. At the time, I did not realize how much I benefited from going to a university where I did not have to worry that I was intellectually capable of being there. I always felt I belonged in my engineering college (Dr. Ronald McNair College of Engineering). Perceptions of perceived inferiority, which so many underrepresented students of color carry with them every day of their college careers, never entered my mind. Of course, throughout my undergraduate college years, I doubted and

questioned myself, but not because I was Black—except for the corporate summer internships.

My summer internships really opened my eyes to the racialized and
gendered perspectives that permeate the STEM industry. About half of
my internship assignments did not even use my engineering knowledge. At one of these companies, I became a glorified event planner
and secretary, with only tokenized instances of engagement with engineering. As it got to be time to make my final project presentation, my
manager hurried me through a brief engineering exercise so my report
would not reflect negatively on his performance as my boss. When I
worked for NASA's Jet Propulsion Laboratory in Pasadena, California,
the internship director took a strong dislike to me and tried to get me
kicked out of my summer internship. Luckily, engineering faculty from
NCAT were also working there for the summer and found out about
her antics; they advocated successfully on my behalf. The director was
upset because my goals for spending my internship money aligned
with my lower-income background (e.g., buy a car, send money to my
mom) and weren't as lofty as my middle-class student peers (e.g., start
a business, design a technological innovation). Because she lacked an
understanding of the plight of students from low-income backgrounds,
she positioned me as wasting the opportunity. In addition, I was subject to frequent comments on my braided hairstyle. It got so bad that
I cut all my braids out and bought a wig. It looked horrible (that was
back in the day when even the Black wigs had Whitish hair texture),
but the comments on my hair stopped. My wardrobe definitely had an
Afrocentric flare, and apparently all the red, black, and green intimi-
dated my colleagues. Yes, my summer internships taught me to expect
my body and my mind to be under attack. Anxiety about these racialized experiences started consuming me as I thought about my postde-
gree employment, but I was very optimistic that once I had the degree,
the STEM world would open up to me. I was wrong.

UPS AND DOWNS IN NEWARK

I received my degree in electrical engineering in May 1996, and in August 1996, I entered the industrial engineering master's program at New Jersey Institute of Technology (NJIT). This master's program came with funding from the GEM Fellowship. GEM recruits high-achieving underrepresented students who pursue master's and doctoral degrees in applied science and engineering. There have been more than four thousand successful GEM Fellows since 1976. NJIT is located in Newark. So, I went from a Black university surrounded by the mostly White city of Greensboro to a university that largely served international STEM students. Forget everything else you've heard about the majority-Black city of Newark—being in Newark was wonderful. Black entrepreneurs lined Broad Street, selling everything from Adidas shoes to hair-care products to construction items. Newark has these twenty-four-hour diners that serve big portions of everything delicious. I lived only thirty minutes from New York City, and Newark has a beautiful park, Branch Brook Park, with an indoor roller-skating rink at its center. I have been an avid roller skater ever since. NJIT offered lots of opportunity for leadership, which I took full advantage of, and I immersed myself in graduate school life. But it's all kind of blurry because I kicked it so hard socially between Newark and New York City. After I graduated with my industrial engineering master's degree in May 1998, I landed my dream job with Hewlett-Packard (HP) as a competitive intelligence analyst. Or so I thought.

Competitive intelligence is the collection and analysis of information to anticipate competitive activity, reverse-engineer competitors' products, and interpret the results to improve on the competing products. HP was experimenting with competitive intelligence as a business strategy for its power products division (AC sources and DC power supplies). It was a tricky position because, if the competitive intelligence analysis did not help the company to develop its business strategy, the failure would be ascribed to me. Every day, in subtle or blatant ways, I was made to feel that I did not belong at my job and was unwanted there. It was not the engineering that troubled my career pathway; it was the way my colleagues treated me. For instance, one engineer put tests and quizzes on my desk as a so-called joke, yet he would stop back later to check my answers. I was the only person he did this to, but I did notice that the darker-skinned Indians appeared to be treated unfairly in comparison with their lighter-skinned counterparts. Some of my colleagues frequently referred to my Black university and my Black body in deficit ways, and my competitive intelligence reports were challenged regularly. I now have the language to describe what was happening to me (e.g., racial microaggressions, racial stereotypes, tokenism, impostorism), but back then, I had not yet developed the understanding that I was being racially abused. I was miserable.

However, I made my fair share of mistakes as well: I way overspent on the corporate account and bought memberships to five culturally affirming organizations in one day (Society of Black Everything). I yearned for a sense of belonging. I was commuting from Chicago to New Jersey, and I once FedExed my roller skates to Newark, using the corporate account, and my boss opened the box. Also, I thought some of my colleagues were being nosy (believe me, a couple of them were), but in hindsight, I can see that some of them really did just want to get to know me. I now realize that the process of developing a relationship with a non-Black person happens differently than I was used to with my mostly Black colleagues and friends. A couple of years later, I got laid off, which basically meant getting fired except that I was entitled to unemployment benefits. After I picked myself up off the floor, I moved back home to Chicago with my three-month-old son, Khari. I decided to use this opportunity to reinvent myself by pursuing a PhD.

STARTING MY RESEARCH

I enrolled in a doctoral program at the University of Illinois at Chicago to understand the experiences of Black students who developed the ability to overcome myriad obstacles and succeed academically in STEM. In my doctoral program, I learned that statistics framing the lives and educational experiences of Black children and adults in deficit-oriented ways were ubiquitous, despite the fact that my experiences and those of many of my college peers contradicted these numbers. I quickly realized that the current research on African American students and STEM education had somehow overlooked my classmates, who excelled in STEM majors. My undergraduate graduating class had over three hundred STEMers, 95 percent of whom were African American. Highly resistant to this narrative, I began taking classes that reinforced my own experiences with Black college students. These classes were mostly taught by Black faculty who had overcome substantial obstacles and showed resilience in their academics and in life. My plans were to understand more fully, and in a principled way, what internal and external factors affected Black STEM college students' identity, success, and resilience. Although my initial experiences with JRF students in STEM disciplines at HWIs gave me a peek at the downside of resilience (e.g., unresolved trauma, strain on mental health, additive stress), the narrative of resilience and high-achieving Black folx was so strong that it diminished the power and the legitimacy of those JRF narratives.

I have had to step outside the mathematics education doctoral program to holistically understand the STEM and life experiences of underrepresented POC. Unpacking STEM education for me began with the acknowledgment that science, technology, engineering, and mathematics are not neutral, objective, unchanging bodies of knowledge. Instead, these fields of human knowledge have been constructed for various purposes, including relegating Black people to the margins of

STEM. Although my degree would be in mathematics education, I also completed graduate coursework in educational psychology equivalent to a master's degree, and I benefited from studying a wide range of perspectives on race, ethnicity, and social inequalities in the United States.

While in the PhD program, I followed in my mother's mathematical footsteps by becoming an adjunct mathematics lecturer at Chicago's Kennedy-King Community College and Harold Washington College. These schools serve an almost entirely African American population. Students entered my classroom burdened with numerous factors that could complicate their educational endeavors, such as being head of their households and working in unskilled occupations, having minimal maternal education, being from a large family (i.e., with a high level of responsibility for siblings), and having frequent encounters with stressful life events (e.g., death of a close relative, incarceration of a family member, alcohol or drug addiction of a close family member, divorce). Yet they believed that a college education could positively change their lives, and for some, it did. But the sad reality for most of the Black students at these community colleges is that the structures of racism are overwhelming and powerful forces, and no amount of academic resilience will counter the omnipresent structures of race (and class, which is a by-product of racism).

Overall, nearly half of all incoming community college students nationwide withdraw within twelve months of enrolling, with Black and Latinx students and the economically disadvantaged (they are often the same students) suspending their educations in even greater numbers. Institutional racism places Black and Latinx students at community colleges at a disadvantage; that is, discrimination manifests in an educational system that penalizes students based on their culture, race, ethnicity, political ideologies, and socioeconomic status.

Educational researchers have often assumed that resilience and perseverance constitute the entire recipe for Black academic success. In my own earlier research on the academic survival of high-achieving Black students, I too had grown accustomed to considering resilience as *the* solution. I now realize that this was done without proper recognition of structural racism, which breeds racist practices, policies, and ideologies that force students to adopt and maintain forms of mental toughness that facilitate their educational advancement. Explorations of racialized social systems—in which economic, educational, political, social, and ideological dynamics routinely advantage White people while producing cumulative and chronic adverse outcomes for students of color—can render deeper understandings of the contexts responsible for the resilience shown by students who are already hampered by a legacy of educational and life inequities. As a result, my research questions evolved from unpacking resilience and its cousin, grit, to understanding the impact of racism.

Racism comes in many flavors: structural, institutional, everyday, color blind, individual, interpersonal, and unconscious (also known as implicit bias). (News flash: although implicit bias exists within all of us, most racism is conscious rather than unconscious, especially in higher education, where faculty, administrators, and staff have opportunities to think deeply about race and racism.) I decided to be more committed to unearthing and disarming the structures of racism, so Black students do not have to be resilient to the point that they compromise their mental and physical well-being. I became determined to investigate the short-term and long-term effects of continually attempting to achieve in an environment where encountering a steady flow of race and gender obstacles is the accepted norm. I began to contemplate how much grit and perseverance is healthy and nurturing. I realize that asking Black students to be resilient without adequate and proper supports (supports that are uniquely designed and implemented with consciousness of racism and gendered racism) is oppression. Currently, we demand that Black students struggle to develop coping mechanisms to safeguard their academic hardiness and provide their own defenses against negative evaluation in toxic educational environments. All the while the STEM environment remains as is, often with very little cultural growth.

AFROFUTURISM, MY NEW VISION IN STEM

The future didn't just happen; it was created.

—*Dr. Mae Jemison*

In the introductory chapter, I talked about envisioning the future through the cartoon show *The Jetsons*. Well, I'm still dreaming about the future of STEM, but the Jetsons are no longer my model of the future. I have finally found the genre that foresees STEM in the future in a way that values my racial identity and intellectual curiosity and creativity. I end this book by describing a future that dismantles conventional thinking, shatters stereotypes, and fills STEM content with imagination and a reconceptualization of the Black scientific identity.

The Black social reality is overdetermined with statistics that put us at the bottom of the well, along with our educational, financial, and medical well-being, thereby creating a sort of demoralizing doomsday outcome for the future of Black people. But there is another world, first envisioned in "Black to the Future."[1] Afrofuturism serves as Black speculative fiction and signification, fused with intelligent science and technological conjecture. Ytasha Womack further defines Afrofuturism as "an intersection of imagination, technology, the future, and liberation" in order to critique not only the present-day dilemmas of people of color but also to revise, interrogate, and reexamine the historical events of the past.[2]

No one does this more extraordinarily than Octavia E. Butler, one of the first Black women Afrofuturist novelists. Her novel *Dawn* posits that nuclear war has led to the end of the human race, which she terms humanicide. During these current times, this fate seems plausible, if the environmental trauma to our planet does not get us first. Butler does something remarkable and powerful: she predicts the future, with prophecies that describe the current STEM landscape with amazing accuracy.[3] Butler's vivid, horror-infused narratives deeply interrogate past and present issues: genetic engineering through the manipulation of organs and subcellular structures to maximize biological enhancements, biotechnology, the trading of human genes, the loss of genetic diversity, the pollution of our ecosystem, the dehumanization of enslaved Black people, sterilization, subordinated racial groups being forced to leave their own homeland, exploring one's genetic heritage (now called DNA testing), and choosing material success at the cost of part of one's own identity.[4]

Despite Butler's much-praised focus on the past, current, and future lives of Black people, she had to accept cover illustrations depicting her Black characters as White.[5] Thus, even in a fictional science-fiction paradigm, her publishers required denial of her characters' authentic racial identity. Her broader mantra expresses the need to embrace and celebrate difference ("otherness") in ethnicities, cultures, and bodies foreign to our own, even if it challenges or shakes up one's ideologies. The experiences for POC in STEM echo Butler's dark and prescient vision: we must accept success at the cost of our own legitimate racial distinctiveness.

The power of Afrofuturism is twofold: (1) POC can see ourselves in the future, alive (a key point, as it's rare to see Black families and communities thriving in mainstream sci-fi) and playing important roles in the STEM knowledge-making process, and (2) exposing the visibility of racism and other isms by baring the dehumanizing tendencies of the dominant group (often White people) on the nondominant group (often POC and aliens). Mark Fisher examines the power and capital that currently exist in the STEM arena, which is manifested in part through science fiction that offers mathematical formalizations such as computer simulations, economic projections, weather reports, futures trading, think-tank reports, and the like.[6] This is shown through futuristic descriptions of science fiction in which technologists and engineers are almost always White or, secondarily, Asian. Thus, most science fiction replicates the racism, sexism, classism, and other discriminatory attitudes that exist in our current reality. Afrofuturism's priority is to recognize that people and places of the African diaspora are vital parts of the future too, and some Afrofuturists claim that they will be the correctors of history in the future.

If I could make accurate predictions about the future of STEM, and if key stakeholders believed in my ability to do so, I would be a billionaire by the end of the year. Butler and other Afrofuturists have shown a powerful ability to predict the world we live in now, but they continue to be undervalued. Kodwo Eshun acknowledged that the value of information about the future circulates as an increasingly important commodity.[7] So as long as STEM continues to be distorted by White male intellectual domination, it will be that much more difficult to envision Blacks or other minoritized people thriving in science, now or later.

Bringing Afrofuturism to the forefront of STEM education has the potential to encourage scientific experimentation while reimagining racial and ethnic identities and changing students' own perspectives about their role in future innovation. Afrofuturism has unearthed the role of science and technology in the lives and futures of Black people from their own perspectives.[8] It projects possibilities for science and technological innovation in the face of formidable human and non-human challenges. Traditional science education curriculum and pedagogy limit the imagination needed for scientific discovery, whereas Afrofuturism teaches us to excite the science imagination.[9] This could easily be fused with digital media, gaming technology, and science labs that include writing, storytelling, animation, and illustration. Afrofuturism has armed me with the ability to dismantle my conventional thinking and shatter my stereotypes (yes, Black folx can harbor stereotypes as well), often inspiring me to reconceptualize my Black STEM identity. This vision of new ways of moving through our collective future, socially, environmentally, politically, and spiritually, has changed me and has the ability to change us all.

I have one final message for all readers of this book, especially my now twenty-one-year-old son, Khari, taken from the trilogy *Xenogenesis*, by Octavia Butler. A mother instructs her young son with these words: "Human beings fear difference . . . Humans persecute their different ones, yet they need them to give themselves definition and status . . . Embrace difference."

NOTES

INTRODUCTION

1. Robbin Chapman, "Rendering the Invisible Visible: Student Success in Exclusive Excellence STEM Environments," in *Diversifying STEM: Multidisciplinary Perspectives on Race and Gender*, eds. Ebony McGee and William H. Robinson (New Brunswick, NJ: Rutgers University Press, 2019).
2. Chapman, "Rendering the Invisible Visible."
3. Ruha Benjamin, "Innovating Inequity: If Race Is a Technology, Postracialism Is the Genius Bar, *Ethnic and Racial Studies* 39 (2016): 2227–34; Ebony O. McGee, "Devalued Black and Latino Racial Identities: A Byproduct of College STEM Culture?," *American Educational Research Journal* 53, no. 6 (2016): 1626–62.
4. Ani Turner and Beth Beaudin-Seiler, *W. K. Kellogg Foundation Report May 2018*, https://altarum.org/sites/default/files/uploaded-publication-files/WKKellogg-MI-Business-Case-for-Racial-Equity-Report_2018.PDF.
5. Ebony O. McGee, "'Black Genius, Asian Fail': The Detriment of Stereotype Lift and Stereotype Threat in High-Achieving Black and Asian Students," *AERA Open* 4, no. 4 (2018): 1–16, doi: 10.1177/2332858418816658.
6. David R. Williams, "Why Discrimination Is a Health Issue," Robert Wood Johnson Foundation, October 17, 2017, https://www.rwjf.org/en/blog/2017/10/discrimination-is-a-health-issue.html.
7. Zinzi Bailey et al., "Racism in the Time of COVID-19," The Interdisciplinary Association for Population Health Science (IAPHS), April 9, 2019, https://iaphs.org/racism-in-the-time-of-covid-19/.
8. Arline T. Geronimus et al., "'Weathering' and Age Patterns of Allostatic Load Scores Among Blacks and Whites in the United States," *American Journal of Public Health* 96, no. 5 (2006): 826–833; Arline T. Geronimus, "The Weathering Hypothesis and the Health of African-American Women and Infants: Evidence and Speculations," *Ethnicity and Disease* 2, no. 3 (1991): 207–221.
9. See Martha Hostetter and Sarah Klein, "In Focus: Reducing Racial Disparities in Health Care by Confronting Racism," The Commonwealth Fund, September 27, 2018, https://www.commonwealthfund.org/publications/newsletter-article/2018/sep/focus-reducing-racial-disparities-health-care-confronting.
10. Jamelle Bouie, "Why Coronavirus Is Killing African-Americans More Than Others," *New York Times*, April 14, 2020, https://www.nytimes.com/2020/04/07/opinion/coronavirus-blacks.html.

11. Michael D. Yates and John Bellamy Foster, "Trump, neo-fascism, and the COVID-19 Pandemic," *MRonline*, April 11, 2020, https://mronline.org/2020/04/11/trump-neo-fascism-and-the-covid-19-pandemic/.

12. See https://iaphs.org/racism-in-the-time-of-covid-19/.

13. Nauseen Hasum et al., "Chicago's Coronavirus Disparity: Black Chicagoans Are Dying At Nearly Six Times the Rate of White Residents," *Chicago Tribune*, April 7, 2020, https://www.chicagotribune.com/coronavirus/ct-coronavirus-chicago-coronavirus-deaths-demographics-lightfoot-20200406-77nlylhiavgjzb-2wa4ckivh7mu-story.html.

14. Fabiola Cineas, "COVID-19 Is Disproportionately Taking Black Lives," *Vox*, April 8, 2020, https://www.vox.com/identities/2020/4/7/21211849/coronavirus-black-americans.

15. See https://iaphs.org/racism-in-the-time-of-covid-19/.

16. Lydia Blanco, "Prior To Covid-19, Dr. Kizzmekia S. Corbett Was Formulating Success As A Black Woman In Science," *Black Enterprise*, April 2, 2020, https://www.blackenterprise.com/prior-to-covid-19-dr-kizzmekia-corbett-was-formulating-success-as-a-black-woman-in-science/.

17. Ibram X. Kendi, "Stop Blaming Black People for Dying of the Coronavirus," *Atlantic*, April 14, 2020, https://www.theatlantic.com/ideas/archive/2020/04/race-and-blame/609946/.

18. Kenya Evelyn, "It's a racial justice issue: Black Americans are dying in Greater Numbers form COVID-19," *Guardian*, April 7, 2020, https://www.theguardian.com/world/2020/apr/08/its-a-racial-justice-issue-black-americans-are-dying-in-greater-numbers-from-covid-19.

19. Janell Ross, "As more black Americans die from coronavirus, community leaders are taking action," *NBC News*, April 17, 2020, https://www.nbcnews.com/news/nbcblk/more-black-americans-die-coronavirus-community-leaders-are-taking-action-n1186256.

20. "Statement on COVID-19 Pandemic," Science for the People, March 25, 2020, https://scienceforthepeople.org/2020/03/25/statement-on-covid-19-pandemic/.

21. Patrick Collison and Michael Nielsen, "Science Is Getting Less Bang for Its Buck," *Atlantic*, November 16, 2018, https://www.theatlantic.com/science/archive/2018/11/diminishing-returns-science/575665/.

22. Dorothy Roberts, *Fatal Invention: How science, politics, and big business re-create race in the twenty-first century* (New York: New Press/ORIM, 2011); Alondra Nelson, *The Social Life of DNA: Race, reparations, and reconciliation after the genome* (Boston: Beacon Press, 2016).

23. Adam Rutherford, "How to Fight Racism Using Science," *Guardian*, January 26, 2020, https://www.theguardian.com/world/2020/jan/26/fight-racism-using-science-race-genetics-bigotry-african-americans-sport-linnaeus.

CHAPTER ONE

1. I capitalize Black and White for racial groups in accordance with American Psychological Association recommendations.

2. National Center for Science and Engineering Statistics, "Women, Minorities, and Persons with Disabilities in Science and Engineering," National Science Foundation, last modified January 2017, https://nsf.gov/statistics/2017/nsf17310/digest/occupation/overall.cfm.

3. Scott E. Page, *The Difference: How the Power of Diversity Creates Better Groups, Firms, Schools, and Societies* (Princeton, NJ: Princeton University Press, 2008).

4. Douglas L. Medin and Carol D. Lee, "Diversity Makes Better Science," *Association for Psychological Science Observer*, May–June 2012, https://www.psychologicalscience.org/observer/diversity-makes-better science.

5. Medin and Lee, "Diversity Makes Better Science."

6. George F. Sefa Dei, "Afrocentricity: A Cornerstone of Pedagogy," *Anthropology & Education Quarterly* 25, no. 1 (1994): 3–28, 5.

7. Sefa Dei, "Afrocentricity," 20; Monica L. Miles et al., "Cultivating Racial Solidarity among Mathematics Education Scholars of Color to Resist White Supremacy," *International Journal of Critical Pedagogy* 10, no. 2 (2019): 98–126.

8. Peggy Gabo Ntseane, "Culturally Sensitive Transformational Learning: Incorporating the Afrocentric Paradigm and African Feminism," *Adult Education Quarterly* 61, no. 4 (2011): 307–23, 308–309.

9. I use the term *underrepresented and racially minoritized* to signify the marginalization and subordination of people of color in US institutions, including colleges and universities. *Minoritized* acknowledges a system of actionable policies and practices that racialize Black, Latinx, and Indigenous peoples, as opposed to the passive *minority* in *underrepresented minorities*, which implies some inherent and normalized state of affairs. Instead, they are rendered minorities by overrepresentation of White supremacy, which actively creates a society that normalizes a hegemonic world view to the detriment of non-White people.

10. Julie Kaomea, "Hawaiian Math for a Sustainable Future: Envisioning a Conceptual Framework for Rigorous and Culturally Relevant 21st Century Elementary Mathematics Education," *H lili: Multidisciplinary Research on Hawaiian Well-Being* 7 (2011): 293, http://www.ksbe.edu/_assets/spi/hulili/hulili_ vol_7/11_Hulili_2011_Vol7_.

11. Jerry Lipka, Dora Andrew-Ihrke, and Eva Evelyn Yanez, "Yup'ik Cosmology to School Mathematics: The Power of Symmetry and Proportional Measuring," *Interchange* 42, no. 2 (2011): 157–83, https://doi.org/10.1007/s10780-011-9153-4.

12. Bev Caswell et al., "We Don't Think of It in Terms of Math, It's Just the Way of Life," in *Annual Perspectives in Mathematics Education: Rehumanizing Mathematics for Black, Indigenous, and Latinx Students*, eds. Imani Goffney, Rochelle

Gutiérrez, and M. Boston (Reston, VA: National Council of Teachers of Mathematics, 2018), 79–92, 85.

13. K. Tsianina Lomawaima and Jeffrey Ostler, "Reconsidering Richard Henry Pratt: Cultural Genocide and Native Liberation in an Era of Racial Oppression," *Journal of American Indian Education* 57, no. 1 (2018): 79–100.

14. Guadalupe San Miguel Jr. and Rubén Donato, "Latino Education in Twentieth-Century America: A Brief History," in *Handbook of Latinos and Education: Theory, Research, and Practice*, eds. E. G. Murillo Jr. et al. (New York: Routledge, 2010), 27–62.

15. Luis C. Moll and Norma González, "Lessons from Research with Language Minority Children," *Journal of Reading Behavior* 25 (1994): 439–56.

16. Norma González, Luis C. Moll, and Cathy Amanti, eds., *Funds of Knowledge: Theorizing Practices in Households, Communities, and Classrooms* (New York: Routledge, 2006).

17. Rubén A. Gaztambide-Fernández, "Decolonization and the Pedagogy of Solidarity," *Decolonization: Indigeneity, Education & Society* 1, no. 1 (2012): 41–67, 47.

18. Mathematics Education Scholars of Color, Registration and Planning Questionnaire, *Proceedings from Mathematics Education Scholars of Color Conference*, May 4, 2018, Chicago, 1.

19. Miles et al., "Cultivating Racial Solidarity."

20. Jesse Washington, "Declining Numbers of Blacks Seen in Math, Science," *NBC News*, October 23, 2011.

21. Lawrence A. Tabak and Francis S. Collins, "Weaving a Richer Tapestry in Biomedical Science," *Science* 333, no. 6045 (2011): 940–41.

22. Catherine Ashcraft and Anthony Breitzman, "Who Invents It? Women's Participation in Information Technology Patenting," 2012 Update, National Center for Women and Information Technology, http://www.ncwit.org/sites/default/files/resources/2012whoinventsit_web_1.pdf

23. "Science Benefits from Diversity," editorial, *Nature*, June 6, 2018, https://www.nature.com/articles/d41586-018-05326-3.

24. Clare O'Connor, "Facebook's 'Pipeline' Excuse: Black Women in Tech Speak Out on Diversity Failure," *Forbes*, July 18, 2016, https://www.forbes.com/sites/clareoconnor/2016/07/18/facebooks-pipeline-excuse-black-women-in-tech-speak-out-on-diversity-failure/#334c260e21d4.

25. Elizabeth Weise and Jessica Guynn, "Tech Jobs: Minorities Have Degrees, but Don't Get Hired," *USA Today*, October 12, 2014, https://www.usatoday.com/story/tech/2014/10/12/silicon-valley-diversity-tech-hiring-computer-science-graduates-african-american-hispanic/14684211/.

26. Lou Silva, "Reconstructing Bermuda's Pipeline for Black Males in Education: From Mazes of Mediocrity to Pathways to Success," presented at International

Colloquium on Black Males in Education: Educational Transitions and Life Trajectories: Bridging Pathways to Success for Black Males, Bermuda College, Hamilton, Bermuda.

27. O'Connor, "Facebook's 'Pipeline' Excuse."

28. O'Connor, "Facebook's 'Pipeline' Excuse."

29. Cary Funk and Kim Parker, "Women and Men in STEM Often at Odds over Workplace Equity," *Pew Research Center Social and Demographic Trends*, January 9, 2019, https://www.pewsocialtrends.org/2018/01/09/women-and-men-in-stem-often-at-odds-over-workplace-equity/.

30. Funk and Parker, "Women and Men in STEM."

31. Ani Turner and Beth Beaudin-Seiler, *W. K. Kellogg Foundation Report May 2018*, https://altarum.org/sites/default/files/uploaded-publication-files/WKKellogg-MI-Business-Case-for-Racial-Equity-Report_2018.PDF.

32. Eduardo Bonilla-Silva, *Racism without Racists: Color-blind Racism and the Persistence of Racial Inequality in America* (Lanham, MD: Rowman & Littlefield, 2018).

33. Bonilla-Silva, *Racism without Racists*.

34. Ebony O. McGee and David Stovall, "Reimagining Critical Race Theory in Education: Mental Health, Healing, and the Pathway to Liberatory Praxis, *Educational Theory* 65, no. 5 (2015): 491–511; Darrell L. Hudson et al., "Are Benefits Conferred with Greater Socioeconomic Position Undermined by Racial Discrimination among African American Men?," *Journal of Men's Health* 9, no. 2 (2012): 127–36.

35. Aldon Morris, *The Scholar Denied: W. E. B. Du Bois and the Birth of Modern Sociology* (Oakland: University of California Press, 2017).

36. W. E. B. Du Bois, *Black Folk Then: A History and Sociology of the Negro Race: The Oxford W. E. B. Du Bois*, vol. 7 (Oxford, UK: Oxford University Press, 2007).

37. Jomo W. Mutegi, "A Critical Examination of the Influence of Systemic Racism in Shaping the African STEM Research Workforce," in *Diversifying STEM: Multidisciplinary Perspectives on Race and Gender*, eds. Ebony McGee and William H. Robinson (New Brunswick, NJ: Rutgers University Press, 2019), https://www.rutgersuniversitypress.org/diversifying-stem/9781978805675.

38. L. R. Thompson, J. L. Davis, and Jomo Mutegi, "'There's No One Here That Looks Like Me': Nation Building as a Response to African American Underrepresentation in the Sciences" (under review).

39. Araceli Espinoza, "The College Experiences of First-Generation College Latino Students in Engineering," *Journal of Latino/Latin American Studies* 5, no. 2 (2013): 71–84.

40. Diley Hernandez et al., "Dismantling Stereotypes about Latinos in STEM," *Hispanic Journal of Behavioral Sciences* 39, no. 4 (2017): 436–51; Diley Hernandez et al., "Latino Parents' Educational Values and STEM Beliefs," *Journal for Multicultural Education* 10, no. 3 (2016): 354–67.

41. Michelle Madsen Camacho and Susan M. Lord, "Latinos and the Exclusionary Space of Engineering Education," *Latino Studies* 11, no. 1 (2013): 103–12.
42. Manning Marable, ed., *Dispatches from the Ebony Tower: Intellectuals Confront the African American Experience* (New York: Columbia University Press, 2000).
43. Rosa M. Jimenez, "Community Cultural Wealth Pedagogies: Cultivating Auto-ethnographic Counternarratives and Migration Capital," *American Educational Research Journal* (2019), doi: 0002831219866148; Miles et al., "Cultivating Racial Solidarity"; Cate C. Samuelson and Elizabeth Litzler, "Community Cultural Wealth: An Assets-based Approach to Persistence of Engineering Students of Color," *Journal of Engineering Education* 105, no. 1 (2016): 93–117.
44. Marvin Lynn et al., eds., *Handbook of Critical Race Theory in Education* (New York: Routledge, 2013).
45. Vincent Basile and Enrique J. Lopez, "Assuming Brilliance: A Decriminalizing Approach to Educating African American and Latino Boys in Elementary School STEM Settings," *Journal of Women and Minorities in Science and Engineering* 24, no. 4 (2018): 361–79; Sarah Rodriguez, Kelly Cunningham, and Alec Jordan, "STEM Identity Development for Latinas: The Role of Self-and Outside Recognition," *Journal of Hispanic Higher Education* 18, no. 3 (2019): 254–72.
46. Elana Curtis et al., "What Helps and Hinders Indigenous Student Success in Higher Education Health Programmes: A Qualitative Study Using the Critical Incident Technique," *Higher Education Research & Development* 34, no. 3 (2014): 486–500; Aaron P. Jackson, Steven A. Smith, and Curtis L. Hill, "Academic Persistence among Native American College Students," *Journal of College Student Development* 44, no. 4 (2003): 548–65.
47. Sarah Omar Alkholy et al., "Convergence of Indigenous Science and Western Science Impacts Student's Interest in STEM and Identity as a Scientist," *Ubiquitous Learning: An International Journal* 10, no. 1 (2017): 1–13; Martin M. Chemers et al., "The Role of Efficacy and Identity in Science Career Commitment among Underrepresented Minority Students," *Journal of Social Issues* 67, no. 3 (2011): 469–91.
48. Cheryl Crazy Bull and Emily R. White Hat, "*Cangleska Wakan*: The Ecology of the Sacred Circle and the Role of Tribal Colleges and Universities," *International Review of Education* 65, no. 1 (2019): 117–41; Julia Maldonado et al., "Engagement with Indigenous Peoples and Honoring Traditional Knowledge Systems," *Climatic Change* 135, no. 1 (2016): 111–26.
49. Jay T. Johnson et al., "Weaving Indigenous and Sustainability Sciences to Diversify Our Methods," *Sustainability Science* 11, no. 1 (2016): 1–11; Sara Tolbert, "'Because They Want to Teach You about Their Culture': Analyzing Effective Mentoring Conversations between Culturally Responsible Mentors and Secondary Science Teachers of Indigenous Students in Mainstream Schools," *Journal of Research in Science Teaching* 52, no. 10 (2015): 1325–61.

CHAPTER TWO

1. Ebony O. McGee, "High-achieving Black Students, Biculturalism, and Out-of-School STEM Learning Experiences: Exploring Some Unintended Consequences," *Journal of Urban Mathematics Education* 6, no. 2 (2013): 20–41.

2. Diversity Stalled; ASEE 2019, https://www.asee.org/papers-and-publications/publications/college-profiles.

3. Joseph Roy, *Engineering by the Numbers, 2018 Edition* (Washington, DC: American Society for Engineering Education, 2019), https://www.asee.org/papers-and-publications/publications/college-profiles.

4. Mohammed A. Qazi and Martha Escobar, "Fostering the Professional Advancement of Minority STEM Faculty at HBCUs," *AACU Peer Review* 21, no. 1/2 (2019), https://www.aacu.org/peerreview/2019/winter-spring/Qazi.

5. Monica Stephens and Zaklya S. Wilson-Kennedy, "A Call for Transformative Leadership: Addressing the Lack of Female Full Professors in STEM at HBCUs," *AACU Peer Review* 21, no. 1/2 (2019), https://www.aacu.org/peerreview/2019/winter-spring/Stephens.

6. National Science Foundation, "Women, Minorities, and Persons with Disabilities in Science and Engineering," National Center for Science and Engineering Statistics, 2019, https://ncses.nsf.gov/pubs/nsf19304/data; Roy, *Engineering by the Numbers, 2018.*

7. NSF, "Women, Minorities, and Disabilities in Science and Engineering."

8. NSF, "Women, Minorities, and Disabilities in Science and Engineering."

9. Stuart Zweben and Betsy Bizot, *2018 Taulbee Survey* (Washington, DC: Computing Research Association, 2019), https://cra.org/wp-content/uploads/2019/05/2018_Taulbee_Survey.pdf.

10. Beth Baker, "Recruiting Minorities to the Biological Sciences: Biologists Are Trying a Range of Approaches to Diversify Their Field," *BioScience* 50, no. 3 (2000): 191–95.

11. William A. Smith, "Black Faculty Coping with Racial Battle Fatigue: The Campus Racial Climate in a Post–Civil Rights Era," in *A Long Way to Go: Conversations about Race by African American Faculty and Graduate Students*, ed. Darrell Cleveland (New York: Peter Lang, 2004), 171–90; William A. Smith, Man Hung, and Jeremy D. Franklin, "Racial Battle Fatigue and the Miseducation of Black Men: Racial Microaggressions, Societal Problems, and Environmental Stress," *Journal of Negro Education* 80, no. 1 (2011), 63–82; William A. Smith, Daniel Solórzano, and Tara Yosso, "Challenging Racial Battle Fatigue on Historically White Campuses: A Critical Race Examination of Race-related Stress," in *Faculty of Color Teaching in Predominantly White Colleges and Universities*, ed. Christine Stanley (Boston: Anker Publishing Company, 2011), 211–38.

12. Ebony O. McGee and David O. Stovall, "The Mental Health of Black College Students: A Call for Critical Race Theorists to Integrate Mental Health into the

Analysis," *Educational Theory* 65, no. 5 (2006): 491–511, doi:10.1111/
edth.12129; Derald Wing Sue, Christina M. Capodilupo, and Aisah M. B.
Holder, "Racial Microaggressions in the Life Experience of Black Americans,"
Professional Psychology: Research and Practice 39, no. 3 (2008): 329–36.

13. Ebony O. McGee, Derek M. Griffith, and Stacey L. Houston II, "'I Know I Have
to Work Twice as Hard and Hope That Makes Me Good Enough': Exploring the
Stress and Strain of Black Doctoral Students in Engineering and Computing,"
Teachers College Record 121, no. 4 (2019): 1–38, http://www.tcrecord.org/
Content.asp?ContentId=22610; "The Voice," https://vialogues.com/vialogues/
play/51836/.

14. B. Lindsay Brown et al., "Understanding Barriers to Diversifying STEM through
Uncovering Ideological Conflicts," in *Diversifying STEM: Multidisciplinary Per-
spectives on Race and Gender*, eds. Ebony O. McGee and William H. Robinson
(New Brunswick, NJ: Rutgers University Press, 2019).

15. Eduardo Bonilla-Silva, "Rethinking Racism: Toward a Structural Interpreta-
tion," *American Sociological Review* 62, no. 3 (1997): 465–80.

16. Brown et al., "Understanding Barriers."

17. Brown et al., "Understanding Barriers."

18. Ruth Enid Zambrana et al., "'Don't Leave Us Behind': The Importance of Mentoring for Underrepresented Minority Faculty," *American Educational Research
Journal* 52, no. 1 (2015): 40–72, 42.

19. Pamela Braboy Jackson, Peggy A. Thoits, and Howard F. Taylor, "Composition
of the Workplace and Psychological Well-Being: The Effects of Tokenism on
America's Black Elite," *Social Forces* 74, no. 2 (1995): 543–57; Adia Harvey
Wingfield and John Harvey Wingfield, "When Visibility Hurts and Helps: How
Intersections of Race and Gender Shape Black Professional Men's Experiences
with Tokenization," *Cultural Diversity and Ethnic Minority Psychology* 20, no. 4
(2014): 483–90.

20. Ebony O. McGee et al., "Black Faculty Tug-of-War between Extra Labor and the
Sense of Responsibility to Serve," in press; Wingfield and Wingfield, "When
Visibility Hurts and Helps."

21. Kevin L. Clay, "'Despite the Odds': Unpacking the Politics of Black Resilience
Neoliberalism," *American Educational Research Journal* 56, no. 1 (2018): 1–36,
27, doi: 10.3102/0002831218790214.

22. Clay, "'Despite the Odds,'" 28.

23. Eduardo Bonilla-Silva, "The Structure of Racism in Color-blind, 'Post-racial'
America," *American Behavioral Scientist* 59 (2015): 1358–76.

24. Eduardo Bonilla-Silva and David Dietrich, "The Sweet Enchantment of Color-
blind Racism in Obamerica," *Annals of the American Academy of Political and
Social Science* 634, no. 1 (2011): 190–206.

25. Bonilla-Silva, "Structure of Racism."

26. Bonilla-Silva, "Structure of Racism."

27. Eduardo Bonilla-Silva, *Racism without Racists: Color-blind Racism and the Persistence of Racial Inequality in America* (Lanham, MD: Rowman & Littlefield, 2018).

28. For example, Zinzi D. Bailey et al., "Structural Racism and Health Inequities in the USA: Evidence and Interventions," *Lancet* 389 (2017): 1453–63; Maya Groos et al., "Measuring Inequity: A Systematic Review of Methods Used to Quantify Structural Racism," *Journal of Health Disparities Research and Practice* 11, no. 2 (2018): 190–205.

29. Ruth Enid Zambrana et al., "Blatant, Subtle, and Insidious: URM Faculty Perceptions of Discriminatory Practices in Predominantly White Institutions," *Sociological Inquiry* 87, no. 2 (2017): 207–32.

30. Ebony O. McGee, "Devalued Black and Latino Racial Identities: A By-product of STEM College Culture?," *American Educational Research Journal* 53, no. 6 (2016): 1626—62.

31. Lee Gardner, "Students under Surveillance?," *Chronicle of Higher Education*, October 13, 2019, https://www.chronicle.com/article/Students-Under-Surveillance-/247312; Janine Jackson, "The FBI Appears to Be Engaged in a Modern-Day Version of COINTELPRO: CounterSpin Interview with Nusrat Choudhury on FBI Targeting of Black Activists," *FAIR*, April 9, 2019, https://fair.org/home/the-fbi-appears-to-be-engaged-in-a-modern-day-version-of-cointelpro/.

32. John Michael Lee and Samaad Wes Keys, "Land-Grant but Unequal State One-to-One Match Funding for 1890 Land-Grant Universities," *OAS Policy Brief*, Association of Public and Land-Grant Universities, September 2013, https://www.aplu.org/library/land-grant-but-unequal-state-one-to-one-match-funding-for-1890-land-grant-universities/file.

33. Peter White, "Rep. Harold Love, Jr. Gets TSU $1.9M for Reparations," *Tennessee Tribune*, April 18, 2019, https://tntribune.com/education/college/hbcu/tsu/rep-harold-love-jr-gets-tsu-1-9m-for-reparations/.

34. James T. Minor, *Contemporary HBCUs: Considering Institutional Capacity and State Priorities: A Research Report* (East Lansing: Michigan State University, College of Education, Department of Educational Administration, 2008).

35. Josh Mitchell and Amanda Fuller, "The Student-Debt Crisis Hits Hardest at Historically Black Colleges," *Wall Street Journal*, April 17, 2019, https://www.wsj.com/articles/the-student-debt-crisis-hits-hardest-at-historically-black-colleges-11555511327.

36. Sara Weissman, "Education Secretary Betsy DeVos Addresses HBCU Leaders about Expired Funding," *Diverse Issues in Higher Education*, October 10, 2019, https://diverseeducation.com/article/157123/.

37. Cary Funk and Kim Parker, "Diversity in the STEM Workforce Varies Widely across Jobs," Pew Research Center, January 9, 2018, https://www

.pewsocialtrends.org/2018/01/09/diversity-in-the-stem-workforce-varies-widely-across-jobs/#fn-24050-26.

38. National Science Board, *Science & Engineering Indicators 2018*, https://nsf.gov/statistics/2018/nsb20181/report/sections/science-and-engineering-labor-force/women-and-minorities-in-the-s-e-workforce.

39. Kristin L. Zeiser, Rita J. Kirshstein, and Courtney Tanenbaum, *The Price of a Science Ph.D.: Variations in Student Debt Levels across Disciplines and Race/Ethnicity* (Washington, DC: American Institutes for Research, 2013).

40. Justin E. Freedman and Beth A. Ferri, "Locating the Problem within: Race, Learning Disabilities, and Science," *Teachers College Record* 19, no. 5 (2017): 1–28; Dorothy E. Roberts, *Fatal Invention: How Science, Politics, and Big Business Re-create Race in the Twenty-First Century* (New York: The New Press, 2013).

41. E. J. R. David and Annie Derthick, *The Psychology of Oppression* (New York: Springer Publishing Company, 2017).

42. Roberts, *Fatal Invention*.

43. Ibram X. Kendi, *Stamped from the Beginning: The Definitive History of Racist Ideas in America* (New York: Penguin Random House, 2017).

44. Ebony O. McGee, "Black Genius, Asian Fail": The Detriment of Stereotype Lift and Stereotype Threat in High-achieving Asian and Black STEM Students," *AERA Open* 4, no. 4 (2018): 2332858418816658.

45. National Science Board, *Science & Engineering Indicators 2018*.

46. Krystal Madden et al., "Cartographies of Race, Gender, and Class in the White (Settler) Spaces of Science and Mathematics: Navigations by Black, Afro-Brazilian, and Pakistani Women," *Diversifying STEM: Multidisciplinary Perspectives on Race and Gender*, eds. Ebony O. McGee and William H. Robinson (New Brunswick, NJ: Rutgers University Press, 2019), 4.

47. Vincent Basile and Enrique Lopez, "And Still I See No Changes: Enduring Views of Students of Color in Science and Mathematics Education Policy Reports," *Science Education* 99, no. 3 (2015): 519–48; David L. Brunsma, David G. Embrick, and Jean H. Shin, "Graduate Students of Color: Race, Racism, and Mentoring in the White Waters of Academia," *Sociology of Race and Ethnicity* 3 (2017): 1–13.

48. Seanna Leath and Tabbye Chavous, "Black Women's Experiences of Campus Racial Climate and Stigma at Predominantly White Institutions: Insights from a Comparative and Within-Group Approach for STEM and Non-STEM Majors," *Journal of Negro Education* 87, no. 2 (2018): 125–39; National Academies of Science, Engineering, and Medicine, *Barriers and Opportunities for 2-year and 4-year STEM Degrees: SySTEMic Change to Support Students' Diverse Pathways* (Washington, DC: National Academies Press, 2016), https://www.nap.edu/catalog/21739/barriers-and-opportunities-for-2-year-and-4-year-stem-degrees.

49. Melissa J. Williams, Julia George-Jones, and Mikki Hebl, "The Face of STEM: Racial Phenotypic Stereotypicality Predicts STEM Persistence by—and Ability Attributions about—Students of Color," *Journal of Personality and Social Psychology* 116, no. 3 (2019): 416–43.

50. Lorenzo D. Baber, "Considering the Interest-Convergence Dilemma in STEM Education," *Review of Higher Education* 38 (2015): 251–70; Lindsey E. Malcom and Shirley M. Malcom, "The Double Bind: The Next Generation," *Harvard Educational Review* 81 (2011): 162–72; McGee, "Devalued Black and Latino racial identities."

51. S. Assari, "Health Disparities due to Diminished Return among Black Americans: Public Policy Solutions," *Social Issues and Policy Review* 12, no. 1 (2018): 112–45; Darrell L. Hudson et al., "Racial Discrimination, John Henryism, and Depression among African Americans," *Journal of Black Psychology* 42 (2016): 221–43; Daphna Oyserman, George C. Smith, and Kristen Elmore, "Identity-Based Motivation: Implications for Health and Health Disparities," *Journal of Social Issues* 70, no. 2 (2014): 206–25.

52. A. Byars-Winston, "Toward a Framework for Multicultural STEM-focused Career Interventions," *Career Development Quarterly* 62, no. 4 (2014): 340–57.

53. Maria Ong, Janet M. Smith, and Lily T. Ko, "Counterspaces for Women of Color in STEM Higher Education: Marginal and Central Spaces for Persistence and Success," *Journal of Research in Science Teaching* 55 (2018): 206–45.

54. UNCF, "HBCUs Make America Strong: The Positive Economic Impact of Historically Black Colleges and Universities," United Negro College Fund, November 14, 2017, https://www.uncf.org/news/hbcus-make-america-strong.

55. National Academies of Sciences, Engineering, and Medicine, *Minority Serving Institutions: America's Underutilized Resource for Strengthening the STEM Workforce* (Washington, DC: National Academies Press, 2019), https://doi.org/10.17226/25257.

56. William H. Robinson et al., "Racial and Gendered Experiences That Dissuade a Career in the Professoriate," *Research in Equity and Sustained Participation in Engineering, Computing, and Technology (RESPECT)* (August 2015): 1–5.

57. Amado Padilla, "Ethnic Minority Scholars, Research, and Mentoring: Current and Future Issues," *Educational Researcher* 23, no. 4 (1994): 24–27.

58. McGee et al., "Black Faculty Tug-of-War."

59. Audrey Williams June, "The Invisible Labor of Minority Professors," *Chronicle of Higher Education* 62 (2015): A32.

60. McGee et al., "Black Faculty Tug-of-War."

61. Kimberly A. Griffin, "Learning to Mentor: A Mixed Methods Study of the Nature and Influence of Black Professors' Socialization into Their Roles as Mentors," *Journal of the Professoriate* 6, no. 2 (2012): 27–58.

CHAPTER THREE

1. Ebony O. McGee, "Devalued Black and Latino Racial Identities: A By-product of STEM College Culture?," *American Educational Research Journal* 53, no. 6 (2016): 1626–62.

2. Ebony O. McGee, Derek M. Griffith, and Stacy Houston II, "'I Know I Have to Work Twice as Hard and Hope That Makes Me Good Enough': Exploring the Stress and Strain of Black Doctoral Students in Engineering and Computing," *Teachers College Record* 121, no. 4 (2019), http://www.tcrecord.org ID Number 22610.

3. Ebony O. McGee and Danny B. Martin, "'You Would Not Believe What I Have to Go through to Prove My Intellectual Value!': Stereotype Management among Academically Successful Black Mathematics and Engineering Students," *American Educational Research Journal* 48 (October 2011): 1347–89, doi: 10.3102/0002831211423972.

4. Ebony O. McGee, "Black genius, Asian fail": The detriment of stereotype lift and stereotype threat in high-achieving Asian and Black STEM students," *AERA Open* 4, no. 4 (2018): 2332858418816658; Dario Cvencek et al., "The Development of Math–Race Stereotypes: "They say Chinese people are the best at math," *Journal of Research on Adolescence* 25, no. 4 (2015): 630–37.

5. Derald Wing Sue et al., "Racial Microaggressions in Everyday Life: Implications for Clinical Practice," *American Psychologist* 62, no. 4 (2007): 271–86.

6. Dario Cvencek et al., "The Development of Math–Race Stereotypes: They Say Chinese People Are the Best at Math," *Journal of Research on Adolescence* 25, no. 4 (2014): 630–37; Laura W. Perna et al., "Identifying Strategies for Increasing Degree Attainment in STEM: Lessons from Minority-Serving Institutions," *New Directions for Institutional Research* 148 (2010): 41–51.

7. Jim Blascovich et al., "African Americans and High Blood Pressure: The Role of Stereotype Threat," *Psychological Science* 12, no. 3 (2001): 225–29; Toni Schmader and Michael Johns, "Converging Evidence That Stereotype Threat Reduces Working Memory Capacity," *Journal of Personality and Social Psychology* 84, no. 5 (2003): 440–52.

8. Scott Plous, *The Psychology of Prejudice, Stereotyping, and Discrimination: An Overview*, n.d., https://www.simplypsychology.org/Prejudice.pdf.

9. Shannon Sullivan, "Inheriting Racist Disparities in Health: Epigenetics and the Transgenerational Effects of White Racism," *Critical Philosophy of Race* 1, no. 2 (2013): 190–218.

10. McGee et al., "'I Know I Have to Work Twice as Hard.'"

11. William A. Smith, "Black Faculty Coping with Racial Battle Fatigue: The Campus Racial Climate in a Post–Civil Rights Era," in *A Long Way to Go: Conversations about Race by African American Faculty and Graduate Students*, ed. Darrell Cleveland (New York: Peter Lang, 2004), 171–90.

12. Sherman A. James, Sue A. Hartnett, and William D. Kalsbeek, "John Henryism and Blood Pressure Differences among Black Men," *Journal of Behavioral Medicine* 6, no. 3 (1983): 259.
13. Sherman A. James, "John Henryism and the Health of African-Americans," *Culture, Medicine, and Psychiatry* 18, no. 2 (1994): 163–82.
14. Gary G. Bennett et al., "Stress, Coping, and Health Outcomes among African-Americans: A Review of the John Henryism Hypothesis," *Psychology and Health* 19, no. 3 (2004): 369–83.
15. Gene H. Brody et al., "Perceived Discrimination and the Adjustment of African American Youths: A Five-year Longitudinal Analysis with Contextual Moderation Effects," *Child Development* 77, no. 5 (2006): 1170–89.
16. Angela L. Duckworth et al., "Grit: Perseverance and Passion for Long-term Goals," *Journal of Personality and Social Psychology* 92, no. 6 (2007): 1087–1101.
17. Ebony O. McGee and Lydia Bentley, "The Troubled Success of Black Women in STEM," *Cognition and Instruction* 35, no. 4 (2017): 265–89.
18. Shirley Mahaley Malcom, Paula Quick Hall, and Janet Welsh Brown, *The Double Bind: The Price of Being a Minority Woman in Science*, AAAS Report 76-R-3 (Washington, DC: American Association for the Advancement of Science, 1976).
19. McGee et al., "'I Know I Have to Work Twice as Hard.'"
20. Ebony O. McGee and Lydia Bentley, "The Equity Ethic: Black and Latinx College Students Reengineering Their STEM Careers toward Justice," *American Journal of Education* 124 (November 2017), http://www.journals.uchicago.edu/doi/full/10.1086/693954.
21. William H. Robinson et al., "Addressing Negative Racial and Gendered Experiences That Discourage Academic Careers in Engineering," *Computing in Science & Engineering* 18 (2016): 29–39, 34, doi: http://ieeexplore.ieee.org.proxy.library.vanderbilt.edu/xpl/articleDetails.jsp?arnumber=7426289.
22. McGee et al., "'I Know I Have to Work Twice as Hard.'"
23. Derek M. Griffith et al., "Cultural Context and a Critical Approach to Eliminating Health Disparities," *Ethnicity and Disease* 20, no. 1 (2010): 71–76.
24. McGee and Martin, "You Would Not Believe."
25. McGee and Bentley, "Troubled Success of Black Women in STEM."
26. Mitchell J. Chang et al., "What Matters in College for Retaining Aspiring Scientists and Engineers from Underrepresented Racial Groups," *Journal of Research in Science Teaching* 51, no. 5 (2014): 555–80; Lorelle Espinosa, "Pipelines and Pathways: Women of Color in Undergraduate STEM Majors and the College Experiences That Contribute to Persistence," *Harvard Educational Review* 81, no. 2 (2011): 209–41; Robert T. Palmer, Dina C. Maramba, and T. Elon Dancy, "A Qualitative Investigation of Factors Promoting the Retention and Persistence of Students of Color in STEM," *Journal of Negro Education* 80, no. 4 (2011): 491–504; Montrischa Williams and Casey E. George-Jackson, "Using and Doing

Science: Gender, Self-Efficacy, and Science Identity of Undergraduate Students in STEM," *Journal of Women and Minorities in Science and Engineering* 20, no. 2 (2014): 99–126.

27. Ebony O. McGee, "Young, Black, Gifted, and Stereotyped," *High School Journal* 96 (2013): 253–63.

28. McGee, "Young, Black, Gifted, and Stereotyped."

CHAPTER FOUR

1. Ebony O. McGee et al., "Black Engineering Students' Motivation for PhD Attainment: Passion plus Purpose," *Journal for Multicultural Education* 10, no. 2 (2016): 167–93.

2. Ebony O. McGee and Lydia Bentley, "The Equity Ethic: Black and Latinx College Students Reengineering Their STEM Careers toward Justice," *American Journal of Education* 124 (November 2017): 1–36.

3. Kenneth D. Gibbs and Kimberly A. Griffin, "What Do I Want to Be with My PhD? The Roles of Personal Values and Structural Dynamics in Shaping the Career Interests of Recent Biomedical Science PhD Graduates," *CBE-Life Sciences Education* 12, no. 4 (2013): 711–23.

4. Dustin B. Thoman et al., "The Role of Altruistic Values in Motivating Underrepresented Minority Students for Biomedicine," *BioScience* 65, no. 2 (2014): 183–88.

5. Andrew G. Campbell et al., "NEST 2014: Views from the Trainees—Talking about What Matters in Efforts to Diversify the STEM Workforce," *CBE-Life Sciences Education* 13, no. 4 (2014): 587–92, 589.

6. Juan C. Garibay, "STEM Students' Social Agency and Views on Working for Social Change: Are STEM Disciplines Developing Socially and Civically Responsible Students?," *Journal of Research in Science Teaching* 52, no. 5 (2015): 610–32.

7. McGee and Bentley, "Equity Ethic," 19.

8. Patricia Frazier et al., "The Relation between Trauma Exposure and Prosocial Behavior," *Psychological Trauma: Theory, Research, Practice, and Policy* 5, no. 3 (2013): 286–94; Ervin Staub and Johanna Vollhardt, "Altruism Born of Suffering: The Roots of Caring and Helping after Victimization and Other Trauma," *American Journal of Orthopsychiatry* 78, no. 3 (2008): 267; Johanna R. Vollhardt, "Altruism Born of Suffering and Prosocial Behavior following Adverse Life Events: A Review and Conceptualization," *Social Justice Research* 22, no. 1 (2009): 53–97.

9. Maya A. Beasley, *Opting Out: Losing the Potential of America's Young Black Elite* (Chicago: University of Chicago Press, 2011), 109.

10. McGee and Bentley, "Equity Ethic," 17.

11. McGee and Bentley, "Equity Ethic," 20–21

12. Kimberly Griffin, "Striving for Success: A Qualitative Exploration of Competing Theories of High-Achieving Black College Students' Academic Motivation," *Journal of College Student Development* 47, no. 4 (2006): 384–400.

13. McGee et al., "Black Engineering Students' Motivation."

14. Christopher Jett and Julius Davis, "Black Males' STEM Experiences: Factors That Contribute to Their Success," in *Diversifying STEM: Multidisciplinary Perspectives on Race and Gender*, eds. Ebony O. McGee and William H. Robinson (New Brunswick, NJ: Rutgers University Press, 2019).

15. Beasley, *Opting Out*, 42.

16. Geoffrey L. Greif, Freeman A. Hrabowski, and Kenneth I. Maton, *Beating the Odds: Raising Academically Successful African American Males* (New York: Oxford University Press, 1998); Sheryl McGlamery and Carol T. Mitchell, "Recruitment and Retention of African American Males in High School Mathematics," *Journal of African American Men* 4, no. 4 (2000): 73–87; Latasha R. Thompson and Julius Davis, "The Meaning High-achieving African-American Males in an Urban High School Ascribe to Mathematics," *Urban Review* 45, no. 4 (2013): 490–517.

17. Senetta Bancroft, "Capital, Kinship, and White Privilege: Social and Cultural Influences upon the Minority Doctoral Experience in the Sciences," *Multicultural Education* 20, no. 2 (2013): 10–16.

18. Orlando Taylor, Jill McGowan, and Sharon T. Alston, "The Effect of Learning Communities on Achievement in STEM Fields for African Americans across Four Campuses," *Journal of Negro Education* 77, no. 3 (2008): 190–202.

19. Taylor et al., "The Effect of Learning Communities on Achievement."

20. Elaine Seymour and Nancy M. Hewitt, *Talking about Leaving: Why Undergraduates Leave the Sciences*, vol. 12 (Boulder, CO: Westview, 1997) 337.

21. McGee and Bentley, "Equity Ethic," 23.

22. Kenneth I. Maton and Freeman A. Hrabowski III, "Increasing the Number of African American PhDs in the Sciences and Engineering: A Strengths-Based Approach," *American Psychologist* 59, no. 6 (2004): 547.

23. McGee et al., "Black Engineering Students' Motivation."

24. McGee et al., "Black Engineering Students' Motivation," 18–19.

25. McGee et al., "Black Engineering Students' Motivation," 16.

26. Clifford Lee and Elisabeth Soep, "Beyond Coding: Using Critical Computational Literacy to Transform Tech," *Texas Education Review* 6, no. 1 (2018): 10–16, doi:10.15781/T24J0BF37.

27. Lee and Soep, "Beyond Coding," 10–11.

28. Michelle Madsen Camacho and Susan M. Lord, *The Borderlands of Education: Latinas in Engineering* (Lanham, MD: Lexington Books, 2013).

29. Kimberley Freeman, Sharon T. Alston, and Duvon G. Winborne, "Do Learning Communities Enhance the Quality of Students' Learning and Motivation in STEM?," *Journal of Negro Education* 77, no. 3 (2008): 227–40, 227.

30. Camacho and Lord, *Borderlands of Education*.

31. Shawn A. Ginwright, "Peace out to Revolution! Activism among African American Youth: An Argument for Radical Healing," *YOUNG* 18, no. 1 (February 2010): 77–96, doi:10.1177/110330880901800106; Julius Davis and Christopher C. Jett, eds., *Critical Race Theory in Mathematics Education* (New York: Routledge, 2019).

32. Geneva Gay, *Culturally Responsive Teaching*, 2nd ed. (New York: Teachers College Press, 2010).

33. Clarence L. Terry, "Mathematical Counterstory and African American Male Students: Urban Mathematics Education from a Critical Race Theory Perspective," *Journal of Urban Mathematics Education* 4 (2011): 23–49.

34. Gay, *Culturally Responsive Teaching*.

35. Terry, "Mathematical Counterstory."

36. Jett and Davis, eds., *Critical Race Theory in Mathematics Education*

37. Tommy J. Curry, *The Man-Not: Race, Class, Genre, and the Dilemmas of Black Manhood* (Philadelphia: Temple University Press, 2017); Alonzo M. Flowers and Rosa Maria Banda, "The Masculinity Paradox: Conceptualizing the Experiences of Men of Color in STEM," *Culture, Society, & Masculinities* 7, no. 1 (2015): 45–60.

38. Dara Naphan-Kingery et al., "How Diverse Engineering and Computing PhD and Postdoctoral Scholars Develop Career Trajectories Principled on an 'Equity Ethic,'" *Journal of Engineering Education* (in press).

39. National Science Foundation, "Women, Minorities, and Persons with Disabilities in Science and Engineering: 2015," Special Report NSF 15-311 (Arlington, VA: NSF, 2015), http://www.nsf.gov/statistics/wmpd/.

40. Mary A. Armstrong and Jasna Jovanovic, "The Intersectional Matrix: Rethinking Institutional Change for URM Women in STEM," *Journal of Diversity in Higher Education* 10, no. 3 (2017): 216–31.

41. Armstrong and Jovanovic, "The Intersectional Matrix."

42. Armstrong and Jovanovic, "The Intersectional Matrix."

43. Maria Ong, Janet M. Smith, and Lily T. Ko, "Counterspaces for Women of Color in STEM Higher Education: Marginal and Central Spaces for Persistence and Success," *Journal of Research in Science Teaching* 55, no. 2 (2018): 206–45.

44. Ong et al., "Counterspaces," 223.

CHAPTER FIVE

1. Lorenzo DuBois Baber, "Colorblind Liberalism in Postsecondary STEM Education," in *Diversifying STEM: Multidisciplinary Perspectives on Race and Gender*, eds. Ebony O. McGee and William H. Robinson (New Brunswick, NJ: Rutgers University Press, 2019).

2. Ebony O. McGee and David Stovall, "Reimagining Critical Race Theory in Education: Mental Health, Healing, and the Pathway to Liberatory Praxis," *Educational Theory* 65, no. 5 (2015): 491–511, doi:10.1111/edth.12129.

3. Lori D. Patton and Stephanie Bondi, "Nice White Men or Social Justice Allies?: Using Critical Race Theory to Examine How White Male Faculty and Administrators Engage in Ally Work," *Race Ethnicity and Education* 18, no. 4 (2015): 488–514, doi:10.1080/13613324.2014.1000289.

4. Craig Steven Wilder, *Ebony and Ivy: Race, Slavery, and the Troubled History of America's Universities* (New York: Bloomsbury Publishing, 2014).

5. Robbin Chapman, "Rendering the Invisible Visible: Student Success in Exclusive Excellence STEM Environments," in McGee and Robinson, *Diversifying STEM: Multidisciplinary Perspectives*, 41.

6. Beatriz Chu Clewell and Shirley Vining Brown, *Project Talent Flow: The Non-STEM Field Choices of Black and Latino Undergraduates with the Aptitude for Science, Engineering, and Mathematics Careers* (Washington, DC: The Urban Institute, 1998).

7. Elaine Seymour and Nancy M. Hewitt, *Talking about Leaving: Why Undergraduates Leave the Sciences* (Boulder, CO: Westview Press, 2000).

8. Lisa Tsui, "Effective Strategies to Increase Diversity in STEM Fields: A Review of the Research Literature," *Journal of Negro Education* 76, no. 4 (2007): 555–81.

9. Tsui, "Effective Strategies to Increase Diversity."

10. Tsui, "Effective Strategies to Increase Diversity."

11. Tsui, "Effective Strategies to Increase Diversity."

12. Tsui, "Effective Strategies to Increase Diversity."

13. Tsui, "Effective Strategies to Increase Diversity."

14. Tsui, "Effective Strategies to Increase Diversity."

15. Sheila Tobias, "Why Poets Just Don't Get It in the Physics Classroom: Stalking the Second Tier in the Sciences," *NACADA Journal* 13 (1993): 42–44, 43.

16. Lawrence E. Carlson and Jacquelyn F. Sullivan, "Exploiting Design to Inspire Interest in Engineering across the K–16 Engineering Curriculum," *International Journal of Engineering Education* 20, no. 3 (2004): 372–78; Daniel W. Knight, Lawrence E. Carlson, and Jacquelyn F. Sullivan, "Staying in Engineering: Effects of a Hands-on, Team-based, First-Year Projects Course on Student Retention," *Proceedings of American Society for Engineering Education Annual Conference*, Nashville, TN, June 2003.

17. Michelle Madsen Camacho and Susan M. Lord, *The Borderlands of Education: Latinas in Engineering* (Lanham, MD: Lexington Books, 2013). For more information, see N. Eleni Pappamihiel and Marcio Moreno, "Retaining Latino Students: Culturally Responsive Teaching in Colleges and Universities," *Journal of Hispanic Education* 10, no. 4 (2011): 331–34.

18. Camacho and Lord, *Borderlands*.

19. Harvey B. Keynes and Andrea M. Olson, "Redesigning the Calculus Sequence at a Research University: Issues, Implementation, and Objectives," *International Journal of Mathematical Education in Science and Technology* 31 (2000): 71–82.
20. Keynes and Olson, "Redesigning the Calculus Sequence."
21. Kenneth I. Maton, Freeman A. Hrabowski III, and Carol L. Schmitt, "African American College Students Excelling in the Sciences: College and Post-college Outcomes in the Meyerhoff Scholars Program," *Journal of Research in Science Teaching* 37 (2000): 629–54.
22. Delece Smith-Barrow, "Successfully Replicating the Meyerhoff STEM Scholars Program," *Hechinger Report*, April 26, 2019; Mariano R. Sto Domingo et al., "Replicating Meyerhoff for Inclusive Excellence in STEM," *Science* 364, no. 6438 (2019): 335–37.
23. Smith-Barrow, "Successfully Replicating the Meyerhoff."
24. Tsui, "Effective Strategies to Increase Diversity."
25. Patricia Gándara, with Julie Maxwell-Jolly, *Priming the Pump: Strategies for Increasing the Achievement of Underrepresented Minority Undergraduates* (New York: The College Board, 1999).
26. Catherine Morrison and Lea E. Williams, "Minority Engineering Programs: A Case for Institutional Support," *NACME Research Newsletter* 4 (1993): 1–11.
27. Tsui, "Effective Strategies to Increase Diversity."
28. Maton et al., "African American College Students Excelling"; Michael F. Summers and Freeman A. Hrabowski, "Preparing Minority Scientists and Engineers," *Science* 311 (2006): 1870–71.
29. Chapman, "Rendering the Invisible Visible."
30. Ruth Enid Zambrana et al., "'Don't Leave Us Behind': The Importance of Mentoring for Underrepresented Minority Faculty," *American Educational Research Journal* 52, no. 1 (2015): 40–72, 52.
31. Zambrana et al., "'Don't Leave Us Behind'"; Tsui, "Effective Strategies to Increase Diversity."
32. Ebony O. McGee, "Mentoring Underrepresented Students in STEMM: Why Do Identities Matter?," in National Academies of Engineering, Science, and Medicine, *The Science of Effective Mentorship in STEMM* (Washington, DC: National Academies Press, 2019), doi.org/10.17226/25568.
33. Dorian L. McCoy, Rachelle Winkle-Wagner, and Courtney L. Luedke, "Colorblind Mentoring? Exploring White Faculty Mentoring of Students of Color," *Journal of Diversity in Higher Education* 8, no. 4 (2015): 225, doi:10.1037/a0038676; Ebony O. McGee, Derek M. Griffith, and Stacey L. Houston II, "I Know I Have to Work Twice as Hard and Hope That Makes Me Good Enough," *Teachers College Record* 121, no. 4 (2019): 1–38.
34. David A. Thomas, "Racial Dynamics in Cross-race Developmental

Relationships," *Administrative Science Quarterly* 38, no. 3 (1993): 169–94; Stacy Blake-Beard et al., "Matching by Race and Gender in Mentoring Relationships: Keeping Our Eyes on the Prize," *Journal of Social Issues* 67, no. 3 (2011): 622–43, doi:10.1111/j.1540-4560.2011.01717.

35. Blake-Beard et al., "Matching by Race and Gender."
36. Zambrana et al., "'Don't Leave Us Behind.'"
37. McGee, "Mentoring Underrepresented Students in STEMM."
38. Kevin L. Clay, "'Despite the Odds': Unpacking the Politics of Black Resilience Neoliberalism," *American Educational Research Journal* 56, no. 1 (2019): 75–110.
39. Michael Ungar, "Put Down the Self-Help Books: Resilience Is Not a DIY Endeavour," *Globe and Mail*, May 25, 2019.
40. McGee, "Mentoring Underrepresented Students in STEMM", Zambrana et al., "'Don't Leave Us Behind.'"
41. McGee, "Mentoring Underrepresented Students in STEMM"; Zambrana et al., "'Don't Leave Us Behind.'"
42. Zambrana et al., "'Don't Leave Us Behind.'"
43. Kecia M. Thomas, Leigh A. Willis, and Jimmy Davis, "Mentoring Minority Graduate Students: Issues and Strategies for Institutions, Faculty, and Students," *Equal Opportunities International* 26, no. 3 (2007): 178–92.
44. Michael A. Hogg, Deborah J. Terry, and Katherine M. White, "A Tale of Two Theories: A Critical Comparison of Identity Theory with Social Identity Theory," *Social Psychology Quarterly* 58, no. 4 (1995): 255–69, doi:10.2307/2787127.
45. Martin N. Davidson and Lynn Foster-Johnson, "Mentoring in the Preparation of Graduate Researchers of Color," *Review of Educational Research* 71, no. 4 (2001): 549–74, doi:10.3102/00346543071004549.
46. Erika D. Tate and Marcia C. Linn, "How Does Identity Shape the Experiences of Women of Color Engineering Students?" *Journal of Science Education and Technology* 14, no. 5–6 (2005): 483–93; Dorian L. McCoy et al., "Colorblind Mentoring? Exploring White Faculty Mentoring of Students of Color," *Journal of Diversity in Higher Education* 8, no. 4 (2015): 225, doi:10.1037/a0038676.
47. Marcus A. Nivet, "Commentary: Diversity 3.0: A Necessary Systems Upgrade," *Academic Medicine* 86 (2011): 1487–89.

CHAPTER SIX

1. Helen Zhao, "What Is a Radical Analysis of Science?," *Jacobin*, July 15, 2019, https://www.jacobinmag.com/2019/07/radical-critical-science-for-the-people.
2. Umair Irfan, "Air Travel Is Surging. That's a Huge Problem for the Climate," *Vox*, January 13, 2019, https://www.vox.com/energy-and-environment/2019/1/11/18177118/airlines-climate-change-emissions-travel.

3. Sam Levin, "Sexism, Racism and Bullying Are Driving People out of Tech, US Study Finds," *Guardian*, April 27, 2017, https://www.theguardian.com/technology/2017/apr/27/tech-industry-sexism-racism-silicon-valley-study.

4. J. P. Mangalindan, "Silicon Valley's Racism Problem Is Bigger Than Facebook," *Yahoo Finance*, December 1, 2018, https://finance.yahoo.com/news/silicon-valleys-racism-problem-bigger-facebook-160224034.html. The Department of Housing and Urban Development announced March 28, 2019, that it is suing Facebook for violating the Fair Housing Act by allowing advertisers to limit housing ads based on race, gender, and other characteristics. The agency also said Facebook's ad system discriminates against users even when advertisers did not choose to do so.

5. Coral Davenport and Mark Lander, "Trump Administration Hardens Its Attack on Climate Science," *New York Times*, May 27, 2019, https://www.nytimes.com/2019/05/27/us/politics/trump-climate-science.html.

6. Susan Scutti, "Here's What We Know about the Fires in the Amazon Rainforest," CNN, August 27, 2019, https://www.cnn.com/2019/08/23/americas/amazon-wildfires-411/index.html.

7. Union of Concerned Scientists, "Cars and Global Warming," https://www.ucsusa.org/clean-vehicles/car-emissions-and-global-warming; Julia Angwin, "Congressman's Bill Would Force Trump Administration to Fulfill Pledge to Study Racial Disparities in Auto Insurance Pricing," *ProPublica*, February 1, 2018; Laura Kirchner, "Federal Judge Unseals New York Crime Lab's Software for Analyzing DNA Evidence," *New York Times*, October 17, 2017, https://www.propublica.org/article/federal-judge-unseals-new-york-crime-labs-software-for-analyzing-dna-evidence; Thomas J. Sugrue, "Automobile in American Life and Society: From Motor City to Motor Metropolis: How the Automobile Industry Reshaped Urban America," http://www.autolife.umd.umich.edu/Race/R-Overview/R-Overview.htm.

8. Jeff Larson, Julia Angwin, and Terry Paris Jr., "How Machines Learn to Be Racist," *ProPublica*, October 19, 2016, https://www.propublica.org/article/breaking-the-black-box-how-machines-learn-to-be-racist?word=Trump.

9. Adam V. Maltese and Robert H. Tai, "Pipeline Persistence: Examining the Association of Educational Experiences with Earned Degrees in STEM among U.S. Students," *Science Education* 95 (2011): 877–907.

10. Katharina Hamann et al., "Collaboration Encourages Equal Sharing in Children but Not in Chimpanzees, *Nature* 476, no. 7360 (2011): 328–31; Felix Warneken et al., "Young Children Share the Spoils after Collaboration," *Psychological Science* 22, no. 2 (2011): 267–73.

11. Michael Tomasello, *A Natural History of Human Morality* (Cambridge, MA: Harvard University Press, 2016).

12. Florence E. Mallon, ed., *Decolonizing Native Histories: Collaboration, Knowledge, and Language in the Americas* (Durham, NC: Duke University Press, 2012); Paul Ortiz, *An African American and Latinx History of the United States* (Boston: Beacon Press, 2018).

13. Michael J. Dumas, "'Losing an Arm': Schooling as a Site of Black Suffering," *Race, Ethnicity and Education* 17, no. 1 (2013): 1–29, https://doi.org/10.1080/13 613324.2013.850412.

14. Cigdem V. Sirin, Nicholas A. Valentino, and Jose D. Villalobos, "Group Empathy Theory: The Effect of Group Empathy on US Intergroup Attitudes and Behavior in the Context of Immigration Threats," *Journal of Politics* 78, no. 3 (2016): 893–908, https://doi.org/10.1086/685735.

15. Carter G. Woodson, *The Mis-Education of the Negro* (Daly City, CA: Book Tree, 2006).

16. Woodson, *Mis-education*, 4.

17. Robert P. Moses and Charles E. Cobb, Jr., *Radical Equations: Math Literacy and Civil Rights* (Boston: Beacon Press, 2001).

18. S. E. Anderson, "Mathematics and the Struggle for Black Liberation," *Black Scholar* 2, no. 1 (1970): 20–27.

19. Anderson, "Mathematics and Struggle," 25.

20. Anderson, "Mathematics and Struggle."

21. Lindsay Perez Huber, "Make America Great Again: Donald Trump, Racist Nativism and the Virulent Adherence to White Supremacy amid US Demographic Change, *Charleston Law Review* 10 (2016): 215–48.

22. Anthony M. Johnson, "'I Can Turn It on When I Need To': Pre-College Integration, Culture, and Peer Academic Engagement among Black and Latino/a Engineering Students," *Sociology of Education* 92, no. 1 (2019): 1–20.

23. Richard Alba and Victor Nee, *Remaking the American Mainstream: Assimilation and Contemporary Immigration* (Cambridge, MA: Harvard University Press, 2009).

24. Nancy S. Landale, R. S. Oropesa, and Aggie J. Noah, "Experiencing Discrimination in Los Angeles: Latinos at the Intersection of Legal Status and Socioeconomic Status," *Social Science Research* 67 (2017): 34–48.

25. Nora R. Garza et al., "Realizing the PROMISE of success for Latinx STEM students" (Laredo, TX: Laredo Community College, 2018), https://library.mentor-connect.org/downloads/488/TXHSIC%20PROMISE.pdf.

26. Sarah Pierce, "Trump Administration's Immigration Executive Orders on Latinos and the U.S. Economy" (Washington, DC: Migration Policy Institute, 2019), https://www.migrationpolicy.org/programs/us-immigration-policy-program/data-and-analysis-related-trump-administration-actions.

27. Sandra L. Colby and Jennifer M. Ortman, "Projections of the Size and Composition of the U.S. Population: 2014 to 2060," US Census Bureau, US

Department of Commerce, March 2015, Washington, DC, https://www.census.gov/content/dam/Census/library/publications/2015/demo/p25-1143.pdf.

28. Ray Barnhardt and Angayuqaq Oscar Kawagley, "Indigenous Knowledge Systems and Alaska Native Ways of Knowing," *Anthropology & Education Quarterly* 36, no. 1 (2005): 8–23, 9.

29. Christine K. Lemley and Tiffany L. Lee, "Honoring Indigenous Teacher Education Students' Stories: Shifting Indigenous Knowledge from the Margins to the Center," *Journal of American Indian Education* 55, no. 2 (2016): 28–50, 31.

30. Barnhardt and Kawagley, "Indigenous Knowledge Systems," 12.

31. Jo-Ann Archibald and Q'um Q'um Xiiem, "Indigenous Storytelling," in *Memory*, eds. Philippe Tourtell, Mark Tourin, and Margot Young (Vancouver, BC: Peter Wall Institute for Advanced Studies, 2018).

32. Nimachia Howe, *Retelling Trickster in Naapi's Language* (Louisville: University of Colorado Press, 2019), 76.

33. Michael D. McNally, "Indigenous Pedagogy in the Classroom: A Service Learning Model for Discussion," *American Indian Quarterly* 28, no. ¾ (2004): 604–617, 607–608.

34. Wendy Berliner and Judith Judd, *How to Succeed at School: Separating Fact from Fiction* (New York: Routledge, 2019).

35. Barnhardt and Kawagley, "Indigenous Knowledge Systems," 9.

36. Marcia Chatelain, "How Universities Embolden White Nationalists," *Chronicle of Higher Education*, August 17, 2017, https://www.chronicle.com/article/How-Universities-Embolden/240956.

37. Shafaq Hasan, "The Case for Reparations to Descendants of Slavery," *Nonprofit Quarterly*, April 28, 2016, https://nonprofitquarterly.org/the-case-for-universities-paying-reparations-to-descendants-of-slavery/.

38. Manisha Sinha, "The Long History of American Slavery Reparations," *Wall Street Journal*, September 20, 2019, https://www.wsj.com/articles/the-long-history-of-american-slavery-reparations-11568991623; Jesus A. Rodriguez, "This Could Be the First Slavery Reparations Policy in America," *Politico*, April 9, 2019, https://www.politico.com/magazine/story/2019/04/09/georgetown-university-reparations-slave-trade-226581.

39. Black Liberation Collective, "The Demands," https://www.thedemands.org/campus-demands.

40. Matt Krupnick, "After Colleges Promised to Increase It, Hiring of Black Faculty Declined," *Hechinger Report*, October 2, 2018, https://hechingerreport.org/after-colleges-promised-to-increase-it-hiring-of-black-faculty-declined/.

41. Robin Starr Minthorn and Heather J. Shotton, eds., *Reclaiming Indigenous Research in Higher Education* (New Brunswick, NJ: Rutgers University Press, 2018).

42. Joni Schwartz, "Faculty as Undergraduate Research Mentors for Students of Color: Taking into Account the Costs," *Science Education* 96, no. 3 (2012): 527–42.

43. Peter LeViness et al., *Association for University and College Counseling Center Directors Annual Survey, Public Version, 2018*, https://www.aucccd.org/assets/documents/Survey/2018%20AUCCCD%20Survey-Public-June%2012-FINAL.pdf.

44. Victoria Nelson, "Addressing Racial Trauma and Hate Crimes on College Campuses," Center for American Progress, August 9, 2019, https://www.american-progress.org/issues/race/news/2019/08/09/473299/addressing-racial-trauma-hate-crimes-college-campuses/.

45. Rakesh Kochhar and Richard Fry, "Wealth Inequality Has Widened along Racial, Ethnic Lines since End of Great Recession," *Pew Research Center* 12, no. 104 (2014): 121–45; Christopher Muller, Robert J. Sampson, and Alix S. Winter, "Environmental Inequality: The Social Causes and Consequences of Lead Exposure," *Annual Review of Sociology* 44 (2018): 263–82; John Gramlich, "The Gap between the Number of Blacks and Whites in Prison Is Shrinking," Pew Research Center, April 30, 2019, https://www.pewresearch.org/fact-tank/2019/04/30/shrinking-gap-between-number-of-blacks-and-whites-in-prison/; Juliana Menasce Horowitz, Anna Brown, and Kiana Cox, "Race in America," Pew Research Center, April 9, 2019, https://www.pewsocialtrends.org/2019/04/09/race-in-america-2019/; Christina Sturdivant Sani, "Homes in Black Neighborhoods Are Vastly Undervalued, Costing Black Homeowners Billions," *Greater Greater Washington*, December 20, 2018, https://ggwash.org/view/70261/the-devaluation-of-assets-in-black-neighborhoods.

46. Adams Nager et al., "The Demographics of Innovation" (2017), https://papers.ssrn.com/sol3/papers.cfm?abstract_id=3066060; Robert Fairlie et al., "The Kauffman Index Startup Activity, National Trends" (2015), http://www.kauffman.org/~/media/kauffman_org/research%20reports%20and%20covers/2015/05/kauffman_index_startup_activity_national_trends_2015.pdf; Jerome S. Engel, *Global Clusters of Innovation: Entrepreneurial Engines of Economic Growth around the World* (Cheltenham, UK: Edward Elgar Publishing, 2014).

47. Rochelle Gutiérrez, "The Sociopolitical Turn in Mathematics Education," *Journal for Research in Mathematics Education* 44, no. 1 (2013): 37–68; Krystal Madden et al., "Cartographies of Race, Gender, and Class in the White (Male Settler) Spaces of Science and Mathematics: Navigations by Black, Afro-Brazilian, and Pakistani Women," in *Diversifying STEM: Multidisciplinary Perspectives on Race and Gender*, eds. Ebony McGee and William Robinson (New Brunswick, NJ: Rutgers University Press, 2019).

48. George Gheverghese Joseph, *The Crest of the Peacock: Non-European Roots of Mathematics*, 3rd ed. (Princeton, NJ: Princeton University Press, 2011).

49. Ivan VanSertima, ed., *Blacks in Science: Ancient and Modern* (New Brunswick, NJ: Transaction Books, 1983).

50. Ebony O. McGee and Lydia Bentley, "The Troubled Success of Black Women in STEM," *Cognition and Instruction* 35, no. 4 (2017): 265–89.

51. Leighton E. Sissom et al., *The Engineering Team: Engineering, Engineering Technologist, Engineering Technician. Annual Report of the Engineer's Council for Professional Development for Year Ending 1978* (1979).

52. Norman Diamond, "The Politics of Scientific Conceptualization," in *Science for the People: Documents from America's Movement of Radical Scientists*, eds. Sigrid Schmalzer, Daniel S. Chard, and Alyssa Botelho (Amherst: University of Massachusetts Press, 2018), 23–28, https://magazine.scienceforthepeople.org/vol22-1/.

53. The Center for the Advancement of STEM Leadership, https://www.advancing-stemleadership.net/.

54. Tonya L. Smith-Jackson and Goldie S. Byrd, "Inclusive Research Excellence: Deconstructing the Research Enterprise to Facilitate Responsible STEM Research," *Association of American Colleges and Universities Peer Review* 21, nos. 1 and 2 (winter/spring 2019), https://www.aacu.org/peerreview/2019/winter-spring/Smith-Jackson.

55. Kelly Mack et al., *Excellence: A Renewed Call for Change in Undergraduate Science Education* (Washington, DC: Association of American Colleges and Universities, 2018).

56. National Science Foundation, *Women, Minorities, and Persons with Disabilities in Science and Engineering*, NSF 17-310 (Arlington, VA: National Science Foundation, 2017), https://www.nsf.gov/statistics/2017/nsf17310/.

57. Smith-Jackson and Byrd, "Inclusive Research Excellence."

58. Scott E. Page, *The Difference: How the Power of Diversity Creates Better Groups, Firms, Schools, and Societies* (Princeton, NJ: Princeton University Press, 2007).

59. Lindsay Brown et al., "Understanding Barriers to Diversifying STEM through Uncovering Ideological Conflicts," in *Diversifying STEM: Multidisciplinary Perspectives on Race and Gender*, eds. Ebony McGee and William Robinson (New Brunswick, NJ: Rutgers University Press, 2019).

60. Lorenzo Baber, "Structuration of Racial Ideology in Postsecondary Education," in *Diversifying STEM: Multidisciplinary Perspectives on Race and Gender*, eds. McGee and Robinson.

61. Robbin Chapman, "Rendering the Invisible Visible: Student Success in Exclusive Excellence STEM Environments," in *Diversifying STEM: Multidisciplinary Perspectives on Race and Gender*, eds. McGee and Robinson.

62. Chapman, "Rendering the Invisible Visible."

AFTERWORD

1. Mark Dery, "Black to the Future: Interviews with Samuel R. Delany, Greg Tate, and Tricia Rose," in *Flame Wars: The Discourse of Cyberculture* (Durham, NC and London: Duke University Press), 179–222, https://www.uvic.ca/victoria-colloquium/assets/docs/Black%20to%20the%20Future.pdf.

2. Ytasha Womack, *Afrofuturism: The World of Black Sci-fi and Fantasy Culture* (Chicago: Chicago Review Press, 2013).

3. Joan Slonczewski, "Octavia Butler's *Xenogenesis* Trilogy: A Biologist's Response," presented at SFRA, Cleveland, June 30, 2000, http://biology.kenyon.edu/slonc/books/butler1.html.

4. Slonczewski, "Octavia Butler's *Xenogenesis* Trilogy."

5. Betsy Mitchell, *Truth Is Change: The Evolution of Octavia Butler's Cover Art* (n.d.), https://theportalist.com/octavia-butler-cover-art.

6. Mark Fisher, "SF Capital," *Themepark* magazine, 2000.

7. Kodwo Eshun, "Further Considerations of Afrofuturism," *CR: The New Centennial Review* 3, no. 2 (2003): 287–302.

8. Reynaldo Anderson, ed., *Afrofuturism 2.0: The Rise of Astro-Blackness* (Lanham, MD: Lexington Books, 2015).

9. Stephanie Springgay and Sarah E. Truman, *Walking Methodologies in a More-than-Human World: WalkingLab* (New York: Routledge, 2017).

ACKNOWLEDGMENTS

OVER THE YEARS, many teachers, fellow researchers, race scholars, mentors, family members, and role models have inspired and encouraged me. Listing all their names and contributions, however, would almost require another chapter. Instead, I will say that I forget none of you and am profoundly grateful to all of you. I would also like to express my deepest appreciation to the hundreds of participants who have nourished me and my research with their narratives and expertise as STEMers of color.

This publication resulted (in part) from research supported by:

National Science Foundation, CAREER Award 06/01/2017–02/28/2022: "The Impact of Racialized Experiences on Doctoral and Postdoctoral Engineering and Computer Science Students of Color STEM Career Trajectories"

National Science Foundation, Broadening Participation in Engineering Division 9/01/2016–8/31/2018: "Coaching toward the Professoriate: Race and Gender Conscious Mentoring for Black Doctoral Students in Engineering and Computing"

National Science Foundation, Engineering Education and Centers Division 3/01/2014–2/28/2017: "Diversity Stalled: Explorations into the Stagnant Numbers of African American Engineering Faculty"

National Science Foundation, Engineering Education and Centers Division 9/01/2014–8/31/2016: "BPE-OT: Beyond the Basics: Race and Gender Conscious Mentoring for Black Faculty Candidates in Engineering"

National Science Foundation Minority Postdoctoral Fellow, 2011–2012: "From Stereotype Threat to Stereotype Management: Successful Blacks and Latinos in STEM"

The content is the sole the responsibility of the author and does not necessarily represent the official views of the NSF.

ABOUT THE AUTHOR

AS AN ASSOCIATE PROFESSOR of diversity and STEM education at Vanderbilt University's Peabody College, I investigate what it means to be racially marginalized while minoritized in the context of learning and achieving in STEM higher education and in the STEM professions. I study in particular the racialized experiences and racial stereotypes that adversely affect the education and career trajectories of underrepresented groups of color. This involves exploring the social, material, and health costs of academic achievement and problematizing traditional forms of success in higher education, with an unapologetic focus on Black folk in these places and spaces. My National Science Foundation (NSF) CAREER grant investigates how marginalization undercuts success in STEM through psychological stress, interrupted STEM career trajectories, impostor phenomenon, and other debilitating race-related trauma for Black, Indigenous, and Latinx doctoral students.

Education is my second career; I left a career in electrical engineering to earn a PhD in mathematics education from the University of Illinois at Chicago, a Spencer Postdoctoral Fellowship at the University of Chicago, and a NSF Postdoctoral Fellowship at Northwestern University. I cofounded the Explorations in Diversifying Engineering Faculty Initiative or EDEFI (pronounced "edify," https://blackengineeringphd.org/). I also cofounded the Institute in Critical Quantitative and Mixed Methodologies Training for Underrepresented Scholars (ICQCM), which aims to be a go-to resource for the development of quantitative and mixed-methods skillsets that challenge simplistic quantifications of race and marginalization (http://criticalscholars4quantresearch.org/). ICQCM receives support from the NSF, the Spencer Foundation, and the W. T. Grant Foundation.

My research has been featured in prominent media outlets, including *The Atlantic, Diverse Issues in Higher Education, The Chronicle of Higher Education, NPR's Codeswitch, The Hechinger Report, Christian Science Monitor, Huffington Post, US News & World Report, Inside Higher Education, Tennessean,* and *The UK Voice Online.*

INDEX

academic advising, 98

active engagement, 88, 100

ADVANCE Institutional Transformation (IT) grant program, 91–92

advocates, 104–105

Afrocentricity, 22

Afrofuturism, 150–153

agribusiness model, 123

Algebra Project, 119

allies, 104–105

allostasis, 56–57, 59–60

Anderson, S. E., 119–120

Asian students, stereotypes of, 54

assimilation, 30, 120–121

associates, 104

battle fatigue, 6, 38, 58–59, 127–128

bias reduction, 128, 135–136

BlackengineeringPhD website, 110

Black people

  equity ethic and, 78–79

  faculty demographics, 35–36

  health disparities, 15–16

  intellectual STEM thought and, 28–29, 118–120

Black resilience neoliberalism, 41–42

Black students, 2–3, 36, 89–90. *See also* underrepresentation in STEM; underrepresented, racially minoritized (URM) students

blind job-match application, 25

brave spaces, 92–93

bridge programs, 100–104

Butler, Octavia E., 150–151, 153

career counseling and exploration, 98

Chancellor's Science Scholars Program, 102

Chapman, Robbin, 104–105

Cineas, Fabiola, 16

classroom culture, 65

climate change, 116–117

clothing, 63–64, 144

code-switching, 63

collaboration, 82–83, 88, 103

college funding, 43–44

college transition, 100–104

Collins, Francis, 24

color blindness

  intersectionality and, 62

  mentoring and, 106–107

  as racism, 7, 39–41

  structural racism and, 42, 46–47, 135–136

  White supremacy and, 26–27

community, importance of, 80–83, 118

community college students, 148

community service learning (CSL), 11, 29, 87, 100

compensation, racial disparities in, 44

competitive intelligence, 145–146

competitiveness, 53–54, 118

coping mechanisms, 8–9, 56–63

Corliss High School, 138–139

counseling centers, 13, 127–128

counterspaces, 92–93

COVID-19, xii, xiii, 14–17

CSL (community service learning), 11, 29, 87, 100

cultural competency, 135–136

culturally responsive teaching, 88–93, 100

curriculum, 99–100

Dawn (Butler), 150–151

discrimination, intersectionality and, 2